British Isles
Weather & Climate

Elements
of
Meteorology

British Isles Weather & Climate

Elements
of
Meteorology

An introduction to the theory of
Meteorology with special reference to
the British Isles

Stephen J Reeve

Snowgoose Books

Contents

Chapter Thirteen - Visual Signs **109**

Locations in the text

Shetland

North West Highlands

Hebrides

A	Aberdeen
BN	Ben Nevis
C	Cardiff
CaM	Cambrian Mountains
CF	Cross Fell
CuM	Cumbrian Mountains
DM	Dartmoor
D	Dublin
Ed	Edinburgh
Ex	Exeter
K	Keswick
IOM	Isle of Man
IOW	Isle of Wight
LD	Lake District

Grampians

BN O Ed

Southern Uplands

Cheviots

CF

Tees Valley

K CuM

LD

Vale of York

IOM

The Wash

ME

Pennines

Galway

Central Plain

Irish Sea

Wicklow Mtns

D

Midlands

Cardigan Bay

CaM

Thames Estuary

V

L

Bristol Channel

C

SE SL

Downs

DM

IOW

Ex PB SCP

Scilly Isles

English Channel

Channel Islands

Western Approaches

L	London
ME	Mersey Estuary
PB	Portland Bill
O	Ochtertyre
SCP	St Catherine's Point
SE	Severn Estuary
SL	Somerset Levels
V	Valentia

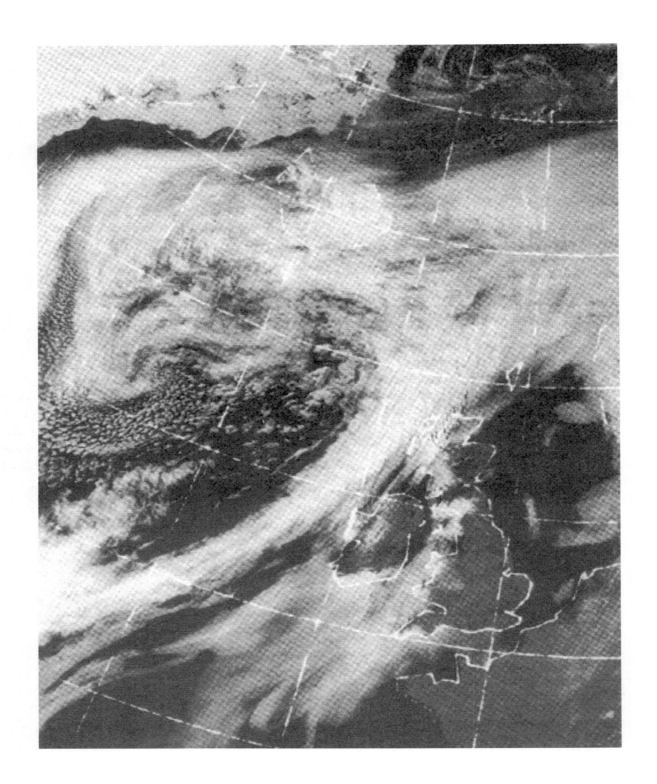

Preface

The daily weather of the British Isles is a frequent topic of conversation and not just because it is constantly changing. The weather is a significant factor in a region where agriculture and fishing remain important, where tourist organisations seek to attract visitors and there is increasing investment in renewable energy especially solar arrays and wind farms, which are weather dependent. The weather at times plays havoc with transport systems as ferries seek shelter from winter gales and snow disrupts the daily routine of even the most efficient airport. 'Leaves on the line' and 'the wrong kind of snow' have long been an ironic comment when reflecting on disrupted rail services and fog still manages to close airports and reduce road traffic to a crawl. Sporting events are at the mercy of the weather with summer sports such as cricket suffering disruption in one of those wet summers that seem to linger in the memory almost as long as the heatwave of 1976. The roof over the Centre Court at Wimbledon has proved money well spent despite a run of generally good summers.

Despite this interest, general understanding of our weather is arguably at an all-time low partly because we have distanced ourselves from the natural world. Not so long ago most folk would look at the sky and have a good idea of what was going to happen within the next few hours. Now we rely heavily on print, broadcast and digital media forecasts so that our own knowledge and reasoning plays little part in predicting how the weather will develop.

A significant reason for the lack of understanding of the natural world in general and weather in particular is change in the school curriculum and the teaching of earth sciences. Traditional education requires the learner to start at the beginning with the basics. From that point, knowledge must be developed through a series of building blocks without the distraction of the thematic approach popular in modern education. All too often in modern texts the human interaction with weather and climate appears long before the student has any real understanding of the physical environment. This is wrong; you cannot begin to understand such interaction until you have a good understanding of elementary meteorology.

The science of meteorology is increasingly driven by number crunching and information technology coupled with the use of sophisticated satellites and supercomputers as researchers attempt to unravel the mysteries of our weather. While this has significantly increased the accuracy of short-term forecasting, it has not led to wider understanding among the public. This book contributes to improved understanding of the drivers of our island weather, demonstrates how forecasts in various formats from a range of sources can help our understanding of the unfolding story in the sky and shows how to use that to predict the weather.

The introduction of more attractive graphics into media forecasts and the involvement of the public with photographic contributions have helped to reinforce the preoccupation with our island weather. However, some would argue that there is a general 'dumbing-down' of weather forecasts aimed at the general public which is perhaps why many were delighted when in a recent television forecast the presenter predicted a wet day and related that to a mass of cloud associated with an occluded front.

This book allows the reader to develop a true understanding of the essential elements of meteorology, which can lead to a lifetime of more detailed study. Using this book as a vehicle to study the elements that drive the weather of our islands the reader can gradually develop an interest in a wider range of related subjects. Once the fundamental principles are grasped readers can, if they wish, take their studies to a higher level or perhaps look at weather as it relates to a range of activities including water sports, aviation, climbing and walking.

You need no previous knowledge of meteorology to benefit from this book. By the end, you will have a body of knowledge that would have served you well for the traditional GCE courses and covers all aspects of present day GCSE courses. You will have a sound understanding of elementary meteorology and have the ability to interpret simple weather maps used in every day forecasting.

This book discusses the elements of weather affecting the geographical area occupied by the UK and Ireland. This is referred to as the British Isles, which is the long established geographical name for the area - Wikipedia and other sources offer many possible variations none of which is particularly suitable. Where possible the text simply refers to the 'islands'.

Throughout the book there are 'British Isles' sections detailing how specific weather elements affect the islands as a whole and more specific regions so as to make the science more relevant.

Cessna 152 at London Southend - meteorology is an important factor in flying

Introduction

The book begins in Chapter One with a discussion of some of the major properties of the atmosphere. This sets the foundation for our study because it is the physical and chemical properties of the atmosphere that determine how the various elements of weather evolve, develop and interact to produce the day to day conditions with which we are so familiar. Although it is beyond the scope of this book it is impossible to understand the winter-spring drought of 2012 and the subsequent cool, wet and windy weather without some appreciation of the characteristics of the atmosphere. In this opening chapter, there is particular emphasis on solar radiation and the resulting energy transfers across the surface. These are central to the study of meteorology because they drive the global air and ocean currents that are a key element in the climate and weather of the British Isles.

The next chapter is a detailed examination of the moisture content of the atmosphere and how that varies spatially and temporally to produce a number of different phenomena. That leads to Chapter Three with an explanation of cloud formation and a description of the major cloud types followed by a brief look at fog in the next chapter.

This part of the book ends with a thorough explanation of how and why pressure varies across the surface of the Earth and how that produces the wind regime of the British Isles. This includes a brief look at local winds such as those found along coasts and in highland areas.

The first part of the book establishes the theoretical background to the elements affecting the weather of the British Isles. Part B builds on this to show how weather systems develop on the atmospheric stage and affect the weather of these islands. Probably the most significant of these systems are the mid-latitude depressions that regularly cross the British Isles bringing wind, cloud and rain. The origin and development of these is considered in Chapter Seven and the resulting weather described at length in Chapter Eight. The following chapter looks at the generation of thunderstorms and their associated weather dominated by thunder, lighting and squally showers.

Air masses and their weather are described at length in Chapter Ten. Although these are clearly not 'systems' they are included here because different air masses with their varied source regions and tracks play a significant part in the formation of depressions. They are also a key factor in the weather associated with a particular depression and indeed the weather of other systems such as non-frontal lows, troughs, anticyclones and ridges.

Part B is completed by a study of anticyclones, which although usually associated with quieter weather than that brought by depressions are nonetheless an important feature of the weather of these islands.

The final part of the book draws together the different elements studied and demonstrates how they can be used in what we might call DIY forecasting. Chapter Twelve shows the reader how to interpret weather charts with twenty different synoptic situations discussed in detail. Chapter Thirteen shows how we can observe visual signs in the sky to predict local weather more effectively. The final two chapters look at the making of commercial forecasts and how they are presented through various media.

winter scenes in Northumberland

Part A

Atmospheric Science

World War II Lancaster enjoying clear skies over the Thames Estuary
Southend-on-Sea Air Show

Part A

Atmospheric Science

This first part of the course provides the background for all weather related studies. No aspect of weather and indeed climate can be understood without reference to the chemical and physical properties of the atmosphere. However, that is a highly complex subject so Chapter One provides just enough information to allow the reader to appreciate the relationship between the atmosphere and various weather phenomena. In effect, this chapter provides the framework around which the rest of the book and your studies are constructed.

The chapter on moisture explains the basic concepts behind condensation, which allow the reader to appreciate the true nature of clouds, which are described in some detail in Chapter Three. There is then a short chapter on the nature of near surface and surface condensation – that is to say fog, dew and frost.

The final two chapters of Part A explain why pressure varies across the Earth's surface and how that leads to airflow including local winds which are such an important part of the everyday weather of the British Isles.

Sadler 25 enjoying a good breeze

meteorology is an important factor in sailing

Chapter One

The Atmosphere

Layers in the Atmosphere

The finite layer that is our atmosphere requires care because it provides us with oxygen and water and prevents extremes of temperature while acting as a shield against harmful solar radiation. Dominated by nitrogen, oxygen and carbon dioxide this mechanical mixture of transparent and odourless gases is so effectively compressed and held to the Earth's surface by gravity that about 50% of its mass lies within 5500 m of the surface and 97% within 30 000 m. A significant effect of this compression is the fall in average density and pressure experienced by mountaineers and by aircraft and space vehicles. The average density of the atmosphere falls from 1.3 kg m^3 at the surface to 0.7 kg m^3 at a height of 5000 m.

The first atmosphere scientists considered the presence of permanent snow and ice at high altitude to be strong evidence of temperature falling with height. However, research dating from the late nineteenth century shows that although the mean temperature falls in the lower atmosphere the air above that is formed of layers within which temperature in the vertical plane alternatively decreases and increases. Nevertheless, temperature allowed the early if crude division of the atmosphere into horizontal zones each having distinct characteristics in terms of temperature, pressure, density and compression and possessing a distinct cap or ceiling formed by a temperature inversion.

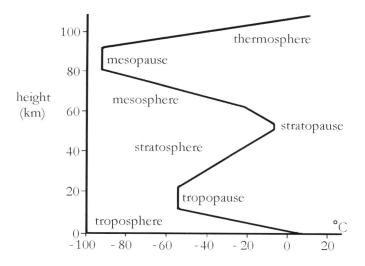

Temperature Inversion

A key characteristic of an inversion is that it acts as a lid on vertical air movement so that in the tropopause it forms a substantial barrier to air attempting to move upwards from the troposphere. In consequence, all the weather that affects our daily lives and virtually all the clouds we see are in this lowest layer of the atmosphere.

> ## *British Isles*

Much early research into the atmosphere took place in the British Isles and occasionally involved as much daring as scientific discovery. Twice in the summer of 1862, the meteorologist James Glaisher and the balloonist Henry Coxwell ascended with a basket full of instruments to about 30 000 feet above the English Midlands in an attempt to discover more about the atmosphere. On the second occasion, they were fortunate to return with their lives.

Troposphere

The troposphere extending upwards from the surface and possessing the greater part of the total mass of the atmosphere including virtually all of the water vapour is of most interest to the weather enthusiast. Capped by the tropopause the depth of this layer varies both spatially and temporally so that its mean height is about 16 km above the equator falling away to only 8 km above the poles.

From the surface to the tropopause, air temperature falls at about 6.5 °C/km. Above that inversion, temperatures no longer fall with height and in certain circumstances, they increase. Moving into the stratosphere temperatures increase with height towards the stratopause. The height of the tropopause and therefore the depth of the troposphere varies with changes in temperature in the troposphere and stratosphere. An increase in temperature at lower levels causes the tropopause to rise, which would also be the result if temperatures in the stratosphere were to fall.

The tropopause is not a complete barrier with exchanges of tropospheric and stratospheric air taking place especially where the mid-latitude jet stream passes close to this layer.

> ## *British Isles*

Above the British Isles, the troposphere is about 8-10 km deep in January rising to 12-14 km in July. However, as with all parts of the mid-latitudes there are daily changes in this height reflecting changes of temperature associated with the passage of areas of high and low pressure.

Radiation

The sun continuously emits vast amounts of energy in the form of heat and light known as radiation with the amount reaching the surface of the Earth varying according to a number of complex factors.

The most obvious is latitude which determines the altitude of the sun above the horizon and the amount of atmosphere through which the energy has passed. Solar radiation striking the surface is more concentrated in the tropics where the sun is directly overhead and the curvature of the Earth more limited. In mid and high latitudes, the oblique rays are more strongly diluted than vertical rays because they pass through a greater depth of atmosphere and the greater curvature of the surface obliges the solar energy to cover a larger surface area. Season is also important in that it determines the length of the day. Another factor is the amount of cloud experienced because where that is relatively high a significant proportion of incoming energy is intercepted.

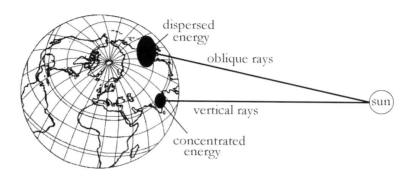

> ### British Isles

Belfast, located halfway between the latitudinal extremes of the British Isles, illustrates some of the factors affecting radiation. Located at 54° 36' N the altitude of the midday sun varies from 35° at the Spring Equinox (20th March, 2015) to a high point of 59° at the summer solstice (21st June, 2015) before falling away through 35° at the Autumn Equinox (23rd September, 2015) to 12° during the Winter Solstice (22nd December, 2015). This demonstrates that for half the year the sun barely rises more than one-third of the way above the horizon and for much of the year is significantly lower.

During the six months between the equinoxes, the total hours of daylight experienced each day rise from about twelve hours at the Spring Equinox to seventeen at the solstice before falling back to twelve hours in September. However, the number of hours each day when the sun is visible on the surface as opposed to hidden by cloud varies tremendously across the islands. In Belfast, the mean annual total is just under 1300 hours (an average of less than four hours each day) which compares favourably with upland areas, which often struggle to pass 1000 hours. However, it is far less than many resorts along the south coast of England, which frequently pass 2000 hours.

Radiation Exchanges

Once solar radiation enters the atmosphere it is subject to a complex range of processes including absorption and scattering by particles in the air and some is reflected directly back to space. Although a significant amount eventually reaches the ground, much of that has no immediate effect on the surface because it is reflected back to the atmosphere as terrestrial radiation. A small amount of that escapes to space but most is redirected back to the surface (back radiation) where it finally provides some warmth.

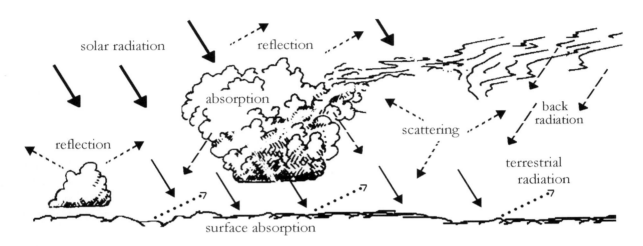

Radiation - Local Exchanges

The mean annual temperature remains relatively constant at a specific location because solar, terrestrial and back radiation and their three-way relationship are relatively unchanged from year to year. As a result, mean temperatures do not vary significantly over a period that may encompass many decades.

➢ ***British Isles***

The presence of a local radiation balance explains why it is possible to state that Valentia (south-west Ireland) has a mean annual temperature of 9.6 °C while that of Ben Nevis (Scotland) is a little under 0 °C. Any change in such figures over a period of several decades would amount to no more than a fraction of a degree.

Radiation - Latitudinal Imbalance

Analysis of the above radiation exchanges at different points on the Earth's surface demonstrates that latitudinally there is no balance. The average annual solar (incoming) radiation is greater than terrestrial (outgoing) radiation between about 30° N and 35° S producing a surplus of solar radiation in low latitudes, which explains why the mean annual temperature for latitude 20° N is 25 °C. By contrast, polar regions receive 250% less annual radiation than the tropics so that north of the Arctic Circle the latitudinal mean temperature is generally in the range 0 °C to -10 °C.

latitudinal variation in the radiation budget

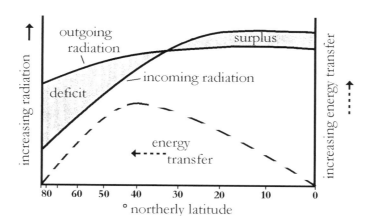

> ## *British Isles*

The mid-latitudes (including the British Isles) receive barely 50% of the solar radiation received in the tropics and because that is considerably less than terrestrial radiation, there is a net deficit of solar radiation. The mean annual temperature for 50° N (the latitude of the south coast of England) is therefore just 6 °C although, largely because of its maritime situation, locations along the English Channel tend to have a mean of 12 °C or more.

Radiation Transfers

It might be expected that mid and high latitudes because they have a heat energy deficit, would over an extended period become progressively cooler while lower latitudes with an energy surplus become warmer. However, research shows that all latitudes retain the same mean annual temperature range from year to year because of a poleward transfer of energy through latitudes 35-40°. This explains the movement of air and water across the surface of the Earth as an attempt to balance areas of surplus heat energy with those that have a deficit.

This energy is transferred by atmospheric and oceanic circulations with the former accounting for about two-thirds of the total although the significance of ocean currents is now recognised through the analysis of satellite photographs and data from oceanic buoys. The imbalance between incoming solar radiation and outgoing terrestrial radiation and the resulting need for energy transfer is the prime driving force behind these currents.

> ## *British Isles*

The British Isles is an area that benefits directly from these transfers with the prevailing westerly winds and the Gulf Stream-North Atlantic Drift transferring heat energy into the mid-latitudes. The mild westerlies and associated frontal systems with their wind, clouds and rain are one of the characteristic features of the climate of these islands. The warm oceanic current particularly during the winter half of the year helps to maintain temperatures well above the latitudinal mean in all parts of the British Isles and allows the west coast of Europe to remain ice free well beyond the Arctic Circle.

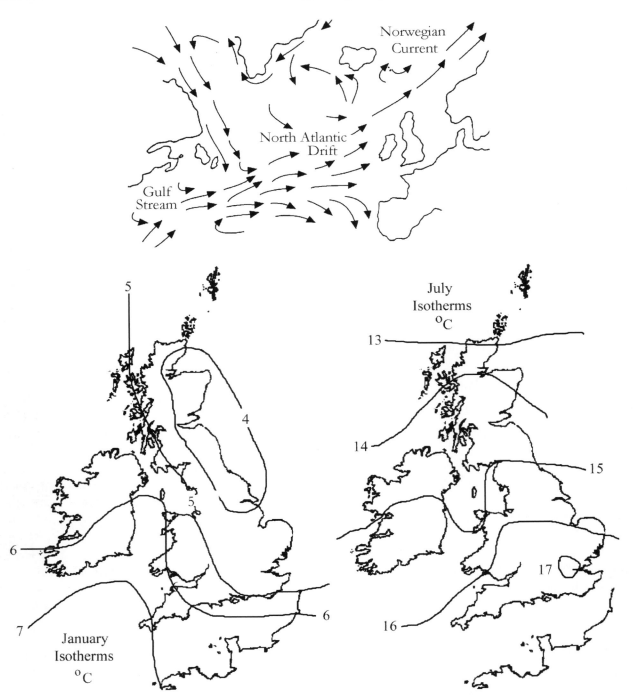

Isotherms trend north to south over the land in winter emphasising the dominance of the westerly maritime influence. Over the sea, they curve north showing that the sea surface is warmer than adjacent land. In summer the isotherms trend east to west across the land indicating that solar altitude (latitude) is the dominant factor in temperature. The 15 °C isotherm curves south over the sea indicating that the sea surface is cooler than adjacent land.

Chapter Two

Atmospheric Moisture

Water

Water existing as a liquid, solid or vapour is an integral part of nearly all meteorological processes and a fundamental requirement of all living systems. It is because a deficiency or excess of water has a major impact on vegetation that the distribution and nature of all ecological systems is determined in part by the availability of water.

➤ *British Isles*

In the British Isles, the relationship between water and environment – albeit with the added influence of human activity – is evident in the contrast between the dusty arable fields of East Anglia and the green pastures of south-west England. It was the lack of rain during the winters of 2010-11 and 2011-12 that in the spring of 2012 forced the authorities to designate parts of central, eastern and southern England as areas of drought. However, the contrary nature of the weather of these islands and especially the variable rainfall regime was emphasised almost immediately by a belt of heavy rain and snow passing southwards across the region although that initially did little to alleviate the developing water shortage. Ultimately, 2012 proved to be the wettest year on record in the British Isles.

Hydrological System

All moisture exists within the global hydrological system and so exists within the hydrological cycle. This consists of several reservoirs the most significant of which are the oceans, atmosphere and ice sheets. Water in its various forms flows through these stores in a complex cycle of transfers and phase transformations.

That the atmosphere holds just 0.035% of all fresh water is surprising given the significance of water in meteorological processes. Near the surface, water vapour comprises 4% of the atmosphere by weight and 3% by volume but above the tropopause, it contributes barely 3-6 ppbv (parts per billion by volume). The vapour pressure of the atmosphere varies with latitude and season with the latter by far the more significant in the lowest 3000 m.

Ocean basins occupied by some 23.5×10^6 km^3 of water hold 97% of all global water. The two major stores of fresh water are groundwater with about 24% of the total and ice sheets and glaciers with 75%. Rivers and lakes contain just 0.3% of all fresh water.

➤ *British Isles*

The precipitation falling at a particular location at any one moment is unlikely to have evaporated from the immediate area. The prime vapour source for precipitation over the British Isles is the atmosphere above the Gulf Stream-North Atlantic Drift and in that regard it is significant that at any moment that air typically has a vapour content equivalent to no more than 10-20 mm depth of water.

The hydrological system is easily observed in the British Isles because the islands are surrounded by ocean. Water evaporated (phase transformation) from the sea surface is swept up into the air as vapour where through the process of condensation (phase transformation) it is formed into clouds that arrive most frequently from the west. Much of the precipitation falling from these is intercepted by vegetation from which varying amounts are returned to the atmosphere by evaporation. Some of the intercepted water eventually reaches the ground adding to that falling directly onto the surface.

Most of the water that does reach the ground percolates into the soil where guided by gravity and slope it enters the fresh water system (lakes and rivers) by which it is returned to the ocean. However, some sinks down through the soil into porous rocks such as the chalk of southern England where it is retained for long periods in aquifers.

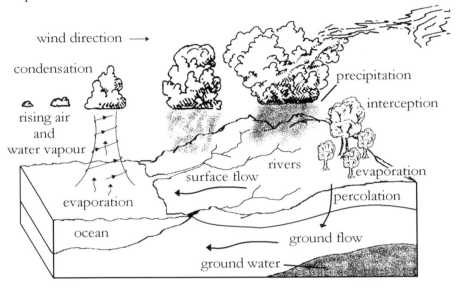

Water Vapour

Water vapour is the invisible gaseous form of water and as far as the weather is concerned, it is the most important of the atmospheric gases. It should not be confused with steam, which is a visible mist of tiny water droplets.

Saturated Air

The maximum amount of water vapour that can be held by a parcel of air is determined by the temperature of that air with the amount it can hold increasing with rising temperature. Conversely, falling temperature reduces the amount of vapour that can be held. At a specific temperature, there is an upper limit to the water vapour that can be held by a parcel of air. When that temperature is reached because of cooling, the air is saturated and the point at which it becomes saturated is known as its dew point temperature. Relative humidity describes the proximity of a mass of air to saturation so that air with a relative humidity of 20-30% is dry while it is moist at 80-90% and saturated at 100%.

In the example below, the water vapour content of a particular mass of air (8 g per kg of dry air) stays constant as the temperature falls from 20° to 10 °C but the relative humidity increases from 52% to 100% at which point the air is saturated. This fall in temperature is either the result of air rising away from the surface or passing over a progressively cooler surface.

temperature	g of water vapour / kg dry air		relative humidity
	air can hold about	actual water content	
20 °C	15 g	8 g	52%
10 °C	8 g	8 g	100%

Condensation

Condensation occurs in the atmosphere when a mass of air reaches its saturation point through one of two processes that frequently work together. One aspect of this is for the vapour content of the atmosphere to increase through evaporation from a large body of water. If the temperature of the atmosphere does not increase at the same time, the relative humidity will increase and the air moves closer to saturation – the effect is similar to adding water to a bucket so that the water surface moves gradually closer to the rim.

simulating addition of water vapour

The second control on relative humidity is changing temperature so that if the air is cooled the total amount of water vapour that can be held falls until relative humidity reaches 100%. To return to the bucket analogy, the size of the bucket is (somehow) reduced while the volume of water inside remains constant. Irrespective of the processes affecting relative humidity, once the dew point temperature is reached (the bucket is full!) water vapour begins to condense onto tiny dust particles and clouds begin to form - our bucket overflows.

simulating air becoming saturated

Condensation Level

The altitude above the surface of the Earth at which a parcel of air reaches its dew point temperature is the condensation level. This can be relatively horizontal for a short distance, which explains why clouds sometimes have a flat base.

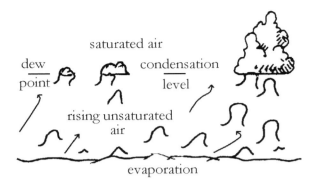

Condensation Nuclei

Experiments show that water vapour requires particles (nuclei) on which to condense. Typically, 0.2 µm in diameter, with large particles reaching perhaps 4.0 µm, these are likely to be sulphur dioxide and smoke over urban areas and wind-blown dust over the countryside. Particles of salt are very important over the oceans and in the westerly maritime air affecting the British Isles, concentrations can reach 10^6 m^3 or even 10^9 m^3. Over industrial conurbations, the figure can be even higher. Soluble nuclei like salt and sulphur dioxide allow condensation when the relative humidity is less than 100%.

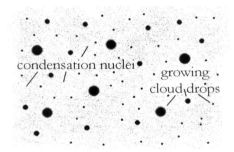

Freezing Nuclei

Condensation drops containing non-freezing nuclei freeze only with difficulty when the temperature falls below 0 °C. Research demonstrates that the formation of ice crystals requires the presence of freezing nuclei especially certain clay minerals and other insoluble materials that are most active at temperatures between -20 °C and -24 °C.

Cloud Drops

Cloud drops exist in a range of sizes although they commonly have a diameter of about 20 µm, which is some one hundred times smaller than the typical raindrop of 2 mm diameter. Only about 1% of clouds produce precipitation because cloud drops and ice crystals are so small and possess such low fall speeds that turbulence invariably prevents them reaching the ground. Additionally a significant proportion of those that do fall below the cloud base evaporate before reaching the ground. One cloud contains insufficient water vapour to sustain prolonged precipitation suggesting that a major thunderstorm observed to produce heavy precipitation for a relatively prolonged period must draw its water vapour from an area measuring more than 1000 km^2.

Raindrops

Cloud drops only fall as precipitation when they have grown sufficiently large to overcome turbulence in the air. The formation of precipitation drops with a diameter of 1-2 mm is a complex process with some growing as initially tiny cloud drops coalesce on collision with similar drops within relatively warm clouds. Eventually drops can reach such a weight they overcome the turbulent updraughts and begin to fall towards the ground.

In cooler clouds, ice crystals (1-5 mm diameter) and supercooled water drops (those with temperatures lower than 0 °C) collide to form ice crystals sufficiently large to fall through the cloud. These reach the ground as either snow or rain depending on temperatures in the lower atmosphere.

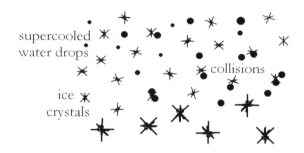

When condensation occurs immediately above the ground, it is defined as fog or mist although the processes are much the same as for cloud formation. This similarity is witnessed whenever low cloud envelops an area of higher ground forming hill fog. When condensation occurs directly onto the ground it produces dew or frost and deposition onto a vertical surface is known as rime.

Cooling

A parcel of air cools either because it has been carried upwards or because it has passed over a cooler surface.

Uplift

Uplift leads to cooling because the air rising away from the surface is subject to progressively lower pressure as there is less depth of atmosphere above it. This fall in pressure allows the air to expand which in turn requires energy acquired from the rising air in the form of heat. There are three prime mechanisms by which air is carried upwards away from the surface and therefore three basic types of precipitation.

Topographic Uplift / Orographic Precipitation

Topographic uplift occurs when air is forced over high ground lying in its path. In this situation, the rising air cools, thereby increasing the relative humidity until dew point is reached, perhaps at an altitude close to the upper slopes of the land. In stable rising air, this produces a widespread mass of cloud embracing the highlands giving rise to a period of sustained precipitation with totals tending to reach a maximum near summits. Once the air has passed the axis of the high ground, it is likely to descend and become warmer with lower relative humidity so that the clouds begin to dissipate and sunny spells become more frequent. The processes and effects on this side of the high ground are the reverse of those on the windward side.

➤ *British Isles*

In the British Isles, orographic precipitation is widespread especially to the north and west of the Tees-Exe line where the landscape is dominated by high ground. Here many upland areas such as the Wicklow Mountains, the Cambrian Mountains and the North West Highlands of Scotland are aligned across the path of the moist westerlies. The air rises above the windward margins of such high ground resulting in high annual rainfall totals even in low-lying locations. Keswick, occupying a valley floor within the Cumbrian Mountains receives an average of nearly 1500 mm each year which is more than two-and-a-half times that of much of eastern England.

The air continues across the broad upland masses before descending the leeward side. In England, the air having passed over the Pennines descends onto the coastal plains of the east where many locations receive little more than 500 mm.

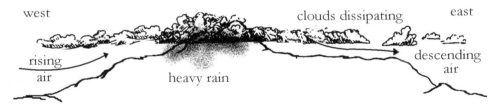

Stable air giving rise to a mass of stratus and nimbostratus over peripheral plains such as those of Cheshire and Lancashire and adjacent valleys and lower slopes can become unstable when forced to rise over higher ground. This gives rise to convective clouds driving up through the layered clouds as the air passes across the high plateau of the Pennines.

When air forced to rise over high ground is unstable the uplift can trigger the formation of cumulus that in favourable conditions grow into cumulus congestus and possibly cumulonimbus. In certain circumstances, these convective clouds become anchored over the higher ground producing sustained heavy rainfall and flash flooding. This was the situation in August 2004 when Boscastle (Cornwall) was devastated by flash flooding as convective cells stalled in their passage across moors close to the village. In a period of less than four hours, 200 mm of rainfall led to flash floods flowing violently down the steep narrow valleys of the area.

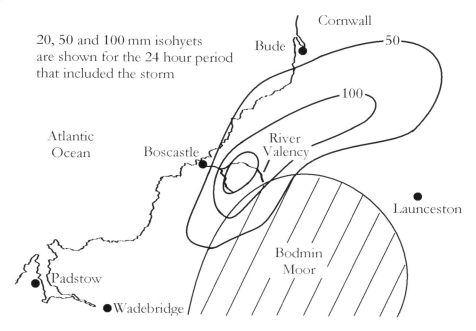

Air Mass Convergence / Frontal Precipitation

When warm and cold air masses meet along a frontal zone there is little mixing because the warm and therefore less dense air is forced upwards and over the colder air. This leads to the expansion of the rising air, cooling and the formation of clouds once the air temperature has fallen to its dew point.

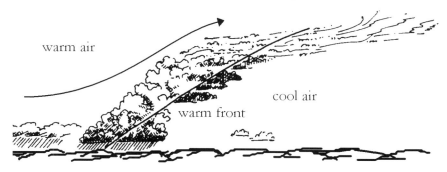

The nature of the cloud associated with a frontal zone depends very much on the incline of the front. The warm front forming the leading edge of a frontal system has a relatively gentle gradient so that the air rising along its slope tends to remain stable producing layered clouds.

The typical cold front is usually very much steeper than a warm front with the warm air ahead of the front being undercut by rapidly advancing cold air. The warm air is forced violently upwards so that it becomes unstable producing large cumulus that may well develop into towering cumulonimbus. This gives rise to a relatively short period of heavy rainfall possibly accompanied by squally winds.

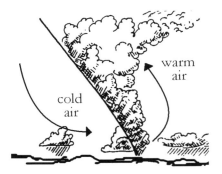

> ### *British Isles*

Air mass convergence produces the widespread precipitation associated with the frontal systems that frequently cross the British Isles especially in the winter half of the year. These produce the greater part of the total precipitation of the islands and virtually all of that in the far north and west.

Thermal Uplift / Convectional Precipitation

Irregular heating of the surface creates hot spots (thermal sources), above which a narrow column of air is less dense than its surroundings and rises in the form of a bubble (thermal). This expands and in doing so uses energy and therefore heat so it cools, possibly to its dew point. When uplift continues far enough above the condensation level it forms a cumuliform cloud that may deliver a shower (diagram, pages 24-25).

> ### *British Isles*

Thermal uplift producing convective rainfall in this way in summer is a common situation over southeast and southern England and the English Midlands because it is those regions that experience the highest surface temperatures. It does occur in others parts of the British Isles including the Central Plain of Ireland during warm spells although with less effect on rainfall totals.

Advection

Advection occurs when relatively warm air passes over a progressively cooler surface so the lowest layers are cooled by conduction and gradually brought to dew point allowing condensation to take place close to the surface. The cooling is gradually spread upwards through the air by turbulence close to the surface. These processes lead either to stratus or advection fog according to the strength of the wind with cloud the dominant feature as the wind increases.

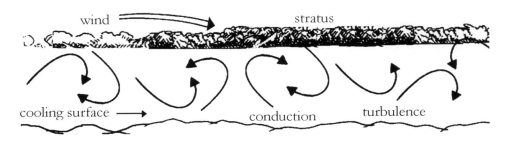

> *British Isles*

In the British Isles, cooling by advection is likely to produce clouds or fog in the Western Approaches and along English Channel coasts at any time of the year. This occurs when tropical maritime air travels over progressively cooler surface waters as it heads north from the Azores.

Along eastern coasts of England and Scotland, a similar effect is likely in late spring-early summer when warm continental air crosses the North Sea where the surface water has yet to warm following the previous winter.

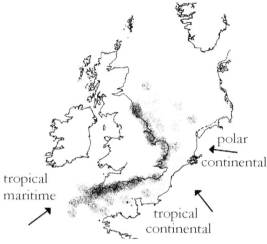

advection fog along the south coast of England

Rainfall (mm / hour)

| 0.01-0.5 | 0.5-1 | 1-2 | 2-4 | 4-8 | 8-16 | 16-32 |

rainfall radar showing band of frontal rain with scattered showers further north

Chapter Three

Clouds

Aggregates of minute water droplets and or ice crystals suspended in the air are grouped into ten cloud genera. Each of these is placed into a group defined according to whether its base is located at low, medium or high altitude and further divided into species some of which are divided into varieties.

base altitude	genera
High (5-13 km)	Cirrus, cirrostratus and cirrocumulus
Medium (2-7 km)	Altocumulus, altostratus and nimbostratus
Low (100 m-2 km)	Stratus, stratocumulus, cumulus and cumulonimbus

Cloud Types

High Base

The three cloud genera seen high in the troposphere, often close to the tropopause, collectively form the cirriform group. High altitude clouds formed of ice crystals appear white because they allow the sun to shine through; they have blurred edges with a fibrous appearance.

Cirrus

Cirrus has an irregular base 8-11 km above the surface. Formed mostly of ice crystals they are thin, white, streaky and often fibrous. Cirrus observed to be hook-like with a distinct head and tail is the species uncinus known as mares' tails in weather folklore. These contrast with the species fibratus, which is a mass of tails without heads.

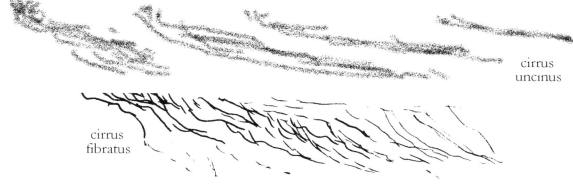

cirrus uncinus

cirrus fibratus

Cirrostratus

Cirrostratus is a whitish veil of fibrous or smooth cirrus covering most or all of the sky. The disc of the sun penetrating through the cloud is usually surrounded by a halo.

Cirrocumulus

Cirrocumulus exists in a number of forms although it is usually seen as a thin white sheet of cirrus broken into lines, ripples or irregular segments. This is referred to as 'mackerel sky' because the markings are similar to the scales seen on certain species of mackerel. Indeed different forms of cirrocumulus are said to resemble different species of mackerel.

> ➤ **_British Isles_**

Cirriform clouds throughout the mid-latitudes are a common indicator of the likely arrival of a frontal system within the next twelve to twenty-four hours.

Medium Base

The three cloud genera at medium altitude are altocumulus, altostratus and nimbostratus.

Altocumulus

Altocumulus occur in several species some of which are only distinguished from cirrocumulus by their altitude. Most forms appear as a mass of rounded segments of varying size either in extensive layers occupying much of the sky or in smaller patches. Sometimes the segments extend into elongated billows and the two forms often appear together in the same part of the sky.

Two particularly attractive forms are the species castellanus and floccus both of which are indicative of unstable air at these altitudes.

floccus   castellanus

Equally pleasing on the eye is the lenticular species that in humid conditions develop in the undulating airflow downwind of a topographical feature. These almond shaped clouds have on occasion been mistaken for UFOs!

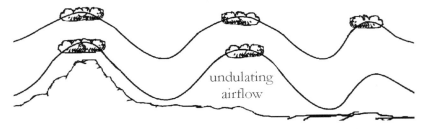

undulating
airflow

➢ *British Isles*

Vivid lightning displays occasionally emanate from castellanus and floccus although this is more likely in the tropics where they can indicate the possibility of lightning closer to the ground but some 50-100 miles distant. In the British Isles, the species altocumulus lenticularis occurs in a number of favoured locations associated with topographical features especially high ground aligned perpendicular to the airflow. The best known of these wave clouds is the 'helm cloud' forming over the summit of Cross Fell in the northern Pennines

Altostratus

Altostratus forming a grey or bluish grey layer 3-4 km above the surface can be fibrous or sheet-like in appearance. Although on occasion the sun is obscured by altostratus, it is more likely to be observed but without a halo and as if seen through ground glass. Light rain or snow can reach the ground from altostratus producing the intermittent precipitation experienced ahead of the more continuous rain associated with the ground position of a warm front.

Nimbostratus

Although nimbostratus is classed as a medium level cloud, it can develop at a range of altitudes down to near ground level. It is unique among the cloud genera in having no species or varieties. A deep, dark mass of cloud obscuring the sun is not formerly classed as nimbostratus unless it is generating precipitation that is observed to reach the ground.

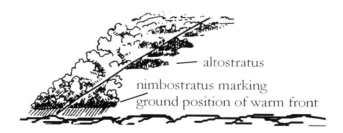

altostratus

nimbostratus marking
ground position of warm front

➢ *British Isles*

Altostratus and nimbostratus are a frequent occurrence in the skies above the British Isles as frontal systems arrive from the west. They usually develop as part of a sequence with the altostratus bringing intermittent light rain, which rarely reaches the ground. Following on behind, the nimbostratus is invariably associated with the threatening dark skies, falling temperatures and strengthening wind ahead of the ground position of a front. They often produce heavy rain lasting for several hours during the passage of a warm front.

Low Base

Low altitude clouds usually appearing dark from underneath because the mass of water drops obscure the sun, can be divided into cumuliform and stratiform clouds. An unstable atmosphere resulting from localised heating and uplift produces tall cumuliform clouds with sharp and relatively well-defined outlines. Featureless layered clouds (stratiform) with diffuse outlines result from the slow widespread ascent of stable air associated with a frontal system.

Among clouds with a low base, the cumulus and cumulonimbus genera form part of the cumuliform group. A key feature of this is that the main species and varieties exist primarily as individual cloud elements rather than appearing as sheets or patches of cloud although it is a common occurrence for a complex situation to develop in which the individual cells merge and lose their separate identity.

Cumulus

When seen from the side cumulus are relatively easy to identify with their typically heaped appearance rising upwards from a flat base. However, when they are directly overhead they are more difficult to identify because the dark ragged base has few distinctive features. In such a situation, they are often confused with a particularly thick mass of nimbostratus.

Initial suggestion of cumulus development is usually the appearance of ragged tufts of cloud (fractus) followed by cumulus humilis commonly known as 'cotton-wool' or 'fair weather clouds'. Although these are quite shallow (wider than they are high) in favourable conditions they can quickly grow into cumulus mediocris, which are roughly as high as they are wide. Continued upward growth leads to cumulus congestus, which with their classic cauliflower or heaped appearance can rise 2-3000 m from a base that is perhaps only 500-1000 m above the surface.

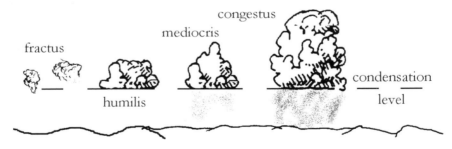

Cumulonimbus

In favourable conditions cumulus develop into cumulonimbus calvus and then capillatus evidenced by the smooth top becoming striated and fibrous at which point it can be 10-12 km above the surface.

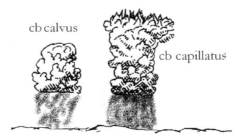

When the top of a cumuliform cloud reaches a stable layer it begins to spread out horizontally with the development of patches of altocumulus cumulonimbogenitus (ac cu gen).

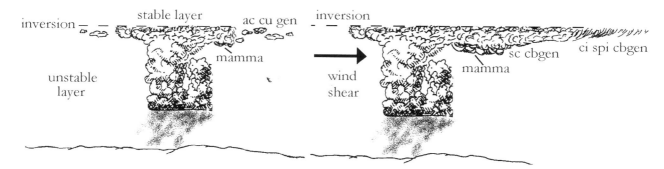

The depth of cumuliform in any given situation is determined partly by the stability of the atmosphere and the height of any stable layer above the condensation level. When strong vertical wind shear (change of velocity with height) is present the top of the cloud is drawn downwind beyond its base to form an anvil shape. When this occurs the ac cbgen tends to merge into thick layers of stratocumulus cumulonimbogenitus (sc cbgen) with the outer edges formed of cirrus spissatus cumulonimbogenitus (ci spi cbgen). This late stage is characterised by mamma (lumpy masses of cloud) hanging vertically downward from the dark undersides of the cloud. Eventually the combined mass of cloud can cover so much of the sky that further convection is prevented and the cloud gradually dissipates.

➢ **_British Isles_**

During a day favouring cumuliform development the mean altitude of cloud base above the British Isles is likely to increase from about 500 m in the morning to 1500-2000 m by mid-afternoon.

Cumuliform clouds develop in situations other than warm summer afternoons over land. In particular, they form day and night in winter in polar maritime air streaming southward towards the British Isles over a warming sea surface as in the visible satellite image below. Throughout the year these clouds can be significant when rapid uplift takes place along a cold front.

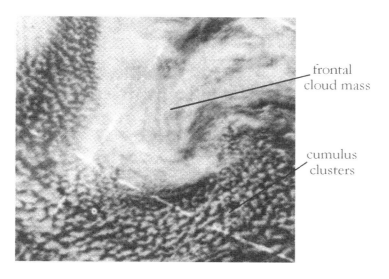

frontal cloud mass

cumulus clusters

Stratus

Among the clouds with a low-level base, stratus and stratocumulus are often referred to as stratiform meaning a cloud that forms a layer across much of the sky.

Stratus is a featureless sheet-like cloud that frequently covers much if not all of the sky. It has a poorly defined base and diffuse outlines through which the sun may on occasion be seen but without a halo. Stratus is most likely to form either as warm air moves over a progressively colder surface or as part of the gradually lifting air within the warm sector of a depression.

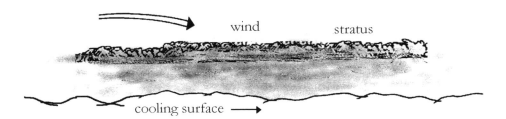

> ### *British Isles*

In the British Isles, stratus is likely to develop when tropical maritime air approaches the south-west coast of the British Isles over a cooling sea. This cooling and the development of stratus is emphasised if such air is then forced by the regional pressure gradient to rise over a topographical barrier such as Dartmoor or the southern edge of the Cambrian Mountains. Extensive sheets of stratus are a common aspect of frontal systems passing west to east across the islands with upland masses like the Pennines often cloaked with hill fog that is simply stratus driven upwards and over the high ground.

Stratocumulus

Stratocumulus is an extensive sheet of grey or whitish grey cloud broken into patches so that the distinct spaces separating the patches give rise to a pattern similar to that of crazy paving or crocodile skin.

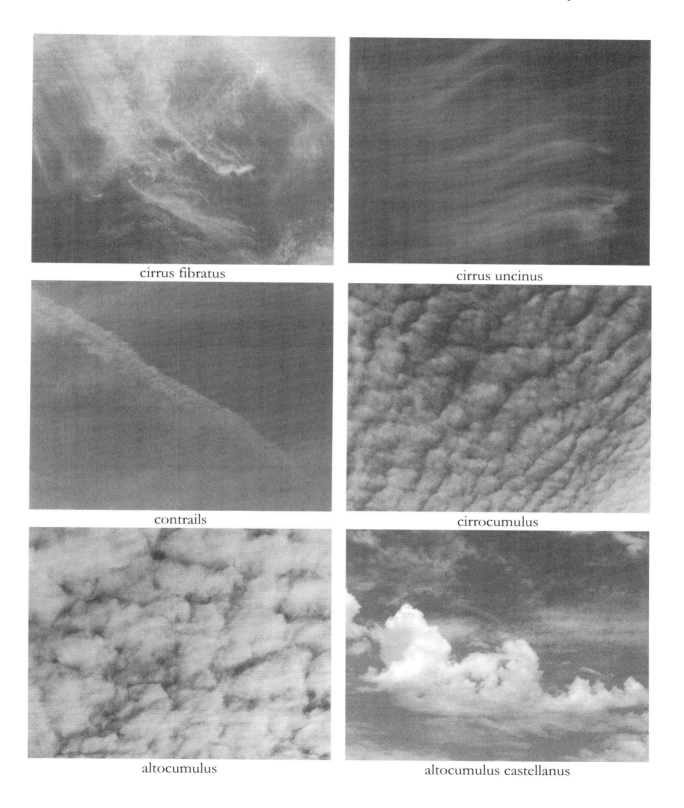

cirrus fibratus

cirrus uncinus

contrails

cirrocumulus

altocumulus

altocumulus castellanus

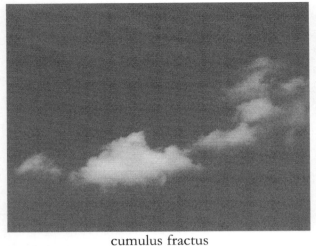

cumulus fractus

cumulus mediocris

cumulus bases over Potton Creek, Essex

Cumulonimbus - January, Newcastle-upon-Tyne

stratus - Gunnislake, Cornwall in July

stratus / hill fog, Cairngorm in June

Chapter Four

Near Surface Condensation

A number of condensation features including fog, dew and frost develop on or close to the surface. All are the result of cooling and condensation in the light wind or calm conditions often associated with the lowest layers of the atmosphere in an anticyclone.

Fog / Mist

When minute droplets of water suspended in the lower atmosphere reduce visibility to 1000-2000 m the condition is defined as mist but if it falls below 1000 m it is fog. There are several different types of fog (and mist), two of which are considered here.

Advection Fog / Mist

Advection fog is the type most likely to affect coastal and offshore waters. It forms when relatively warm moist air passes across a body of water whose temperature is below the dew point temperature of the air. The sea lowers the temperature of the surface layer of the air to its dew point resulting in condensation and fog formation in the lowest layers unless the wind is more than a gentle breeze in which case stratus forms.

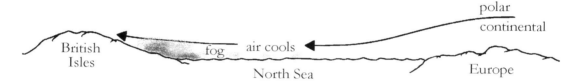

> ### British Isles

Advection fog is especially likely in late spring-early summer when the temperature gradient between land and sea reaches its maximum. Ideal conditions for the formation of fog in the English Channel are the passage of a tropical maritime air mass from the south-west across the Western Approaches and into the Channel. Along the east coast reduced visibility is likely when a continental air mass from Europe

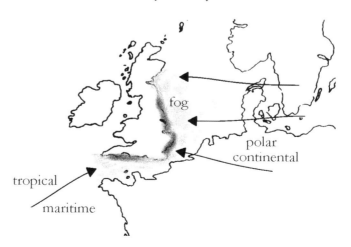

picks up moisture while being cooled by its passage across the North Sea in early summer. This leads to fog formation along the east coast and is responsible for the notorious sea frets and haar.

Warkworth Castle, Northumberland seen across a fret occupying Alnmouth Bay

Radiation Fog / Mist

Under the clear skies of an anticyclone, the land cools rapidly at night. This in turn cools the lowest part of the air leading to condensation that is spread upwards by turbulence to produce radiation fog if the wind is relatively light. On those occasions when the wind exceeds 7-10 mph the cooling is spread higher and relatively weakly so that stratus forms rather than fog. In the absence of wind and therefore turbulence, any condensation will be deposited as dew (frost in winter) rather than fog.

Radiation fog can persist for several days in winter but in summer is dispersed relatively rapidly after dawn. Although forming only over land this fog can drift across coastal waters particularly where a broad estuary is surrounded by a wide expanse of saltmarsh.

➤ *British Isles*

In the British Isles as elsewhere, the development of radiation fog is encouraged by a mix of cold air drainage and a wetland landscape. Areas that are particularly prone to fog include the Somerset Levels, parts of the Vale of York and the lower Tees valley in England. In contrast, locations such as Valentia on the south-west coast of Ireland and fully exposed to the westerly airflow have few days of radiation fog.

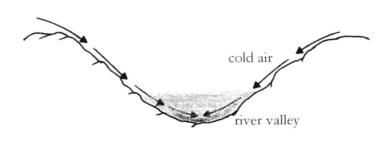

radiation fog occupying a valley floor – seen from above

Dew

Dew formation is encouraged by clear skies, moist air and no more than a gentle breeze close to the surface. Under clear skies, the Earth rapidly loses heat and cools the air immediately above the surface to its dew point. Condensation from this saturated air forms on surfaces facing outward from the ground with grass and plant leaves providing the necessary nuclei.

Frost

When the temperature continues to fall it may reach a point where frost begins to form although this is a surprisingly complex process. Forecasters frequently refer to air and ground frost with the former measured at a height of 1.25 m above the ground whereas ground frost occurs when that temperature is recorded on a grass surface 5 cm above the ground. The result is an icy surface with grass stems and smaller leaves becoming harder than might otherwise be expected.

In circumstances where the air does not become saturated until its temperature has fallen below 0 °C the water vapour condenses directly as fine icy deposits known as hoar frost. When initial condensation on the ground with temperatures above freezing produces dew, this subsequently forms hoar frost if temperatures later fall below 0 °C. Following a particularly cold night the white feathery tentacles of hoar frost may produce such a thick layer that at first glance it would seem as if snow has fallen.

In the freezing conditions described above supercooled liquid fog drops driven by the wind are likely to freeze onto vertical objects such as trees or lampposts producing rime.

frosty meadow

wings need to be de-iced before take-off!

Chapter Five

Pressure and Wind

Pressure

The latitudinal variation in the mean temperature of the Earth's surface has an effect on the overlying air and interaction at this interface is responsible for much of our weather. Where air is in contact with a warm surface, its lowest layers are warmed by conduction from that surface. The warmed air expands and becoming less dense begins to rise and carries heat upwards by convection. In rising away from the surface, the air lessens the force pressing down on the surface creating an area of lower pressure. Above a cold surface the reverse takes place with the lower atmosphere cooled by the surface sinking downwards and increasing pressure on that surface forming an area of higher pressure.

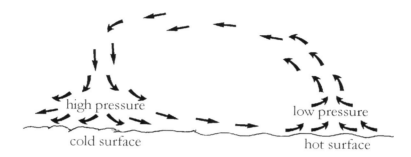

The force of gravity pulling down on air molecules creates a downward force known as atmospheric pressure, which can be measured at any altitude including the Earth's surface where it exerts a force per unit area on that surface. The standard unit of measurement is the hectopascal (hPa) or more commonly millibar with a sea level pressure of 1000 mb (1000 hPa) being equal to a reading of 29.5 inches on a traditional barometer.

The mean sea level pressure over the Earth's surface is 1013 mb (equivalent to 10 000 kg/m^2) although that hides massive regional variations with extensive areas dominated by permanent or near permanent areas of high or low pressure. Areas of the surface that are particularly warm or cold for long periods develop their own pressure characteristics so that in general a warm surface generates low pressure and a cold surface generates high pressure. That this is a generalisation is emphasised by the presence of high pressure over North Africa during the northern hemisphere winter.

➢ *British Isles*

There are no permanent or even semi-permanent areas of high or low pressure close to the British Isles, which is very much a transitional area dominated by travelling areas of high and low pressure. Far to the south, the Azores high pressure forming part of the global sub-tropical high pressure belt persists throughout the year. This is the source for the south-westerly flow that frequently crosses the British Isles. In winter, the intense Icelandic low pressure extends westward to the southern tip of Greenland but in summer is far less evident. To the east, there is no significant pressure cell until well east of the Urals, where in winter the central Asian high pressure is dominant but fades away in summer. To the west of the British Isles, there is no fixed pressure cell until the Americas are reached with an intense high pressure cell over North America in winter that weakens in summer.

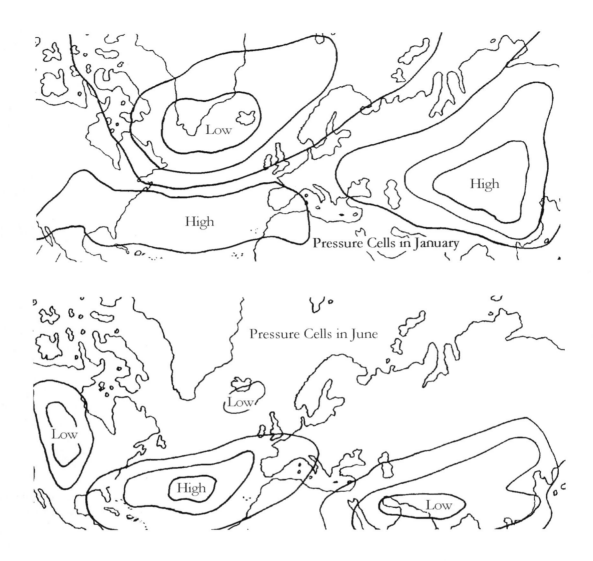

The highest pressure recorded in the British Isles is 1053.6 mb at Aberdeen on 31st January 1902 and the lowest pressure, 925.6 mb, was recorded at Ochtertyre, near Crieff, Perthshire on 26th January 1884.

Wind

As pressure varies across the surface of the Earth, the intensity of the pressure gradient between two areas of differing pressure can be measured to produce the horizontal pressure gradient force. Air moves along this gradient always from high to lower pressure with a strength that is proportional to the gradient. This strength or velocity is usually measured in ms (metres per second) although knots, mph and kph are also used so that

1 ms = 3.6 kph = 1.94 kt = 2.24 mph

Throughout the British Isles, forecasters continue to use the Beaufort Scale (Appendix 3) when predicting wind strengths in coastal and offshore waters. This allows the observer to compare a range of descriptions to a numerical wind scale to determine the approximate speed of the wind at any given moment.

Mapping Pressure and Wind

A key aspect of weather forecasting is the conversion of data from weather stations into maps displaying weather systems allowing professionals and the public to predict the weather.

Isobars

The horizontal pressure gradient is mapped by isobars joining points of equal pressure with a constant interval, usually 4 mb or 8 mb, between successive lines. Where the lines are close together the pressure gradient is steep causing rapid acceleration and strong winds while the reverse is true where they are widely spaced. The maximum rate of pressure change occurs at right angles to the lines.

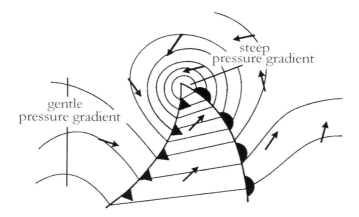

Surface inflow into an area of low pressure has to be balanced by uplift and outflow at higher altitude otherwise the low pressure would fill. Equally, the descent of air into a surface high pressure has to be matched by divergence at the surface.

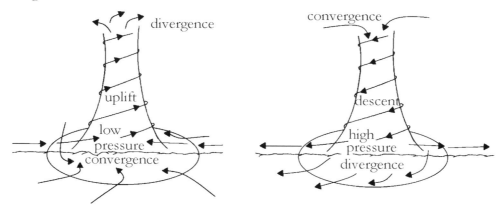

Isobars have smooth curves except near fronts where they change direction abruptly indicating an equally abrupt change in wind direction.

Enclosed isobars are found around centres of high and low pressure. An elongated extension away from a high pressure centre is a ridge (page 74) whereas away from a low pressure centre it is a trough (page 52). Areas of almost constant pressure between high and low pressure known as cols are indicated by an area lacking isobars.

Surface and High Altitude Flows

The air at different altitudes through the troposphere is often found to be flowing at different speeds and in different directions as it responds to a number of controlling factors.

Buys Ballot

Factors other than the pressure gradient force act on the air otherwise the flow would be unbalanced and rush towards the low pressure. Such flow is impossible and proved not to exist by the evidence of actual flows showing that air does not flow directly from high to low pressure. The Dutch scientist Buys Ballot (1857) demonstrated that if in the northern hemisphere you stand with your back to the wind the lower pressure is to your left and higher pressure to the right in which case the air is not flowing directly from one to the other. In the southern hemisphere, lower pressure is on your right and the higher pressure is to your left.

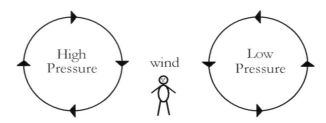

Coriolis Force

Air does not flow directly between high and low pressure for a number of reasons. One involves the rotation of the Earth, which causes the Coriolis Force to act at right angles to moving air (or water) so that it is effectively pushed sideways while continuing to move forward. The west to east rotation of the Earth causes any mass moving across the surface to be deflected so that it flows at an angle to the pressure gradient. In the northern hemisphere, this deflection forces air (at any altitude) or water (at any depth) to curve to the right of its path while in the southern hemisphere it curves to the left.

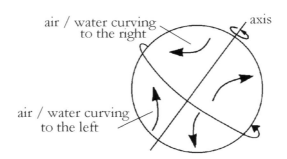

> ➤ *British Isles*

Without such a deflection, the south-westerlies that frequently affect the British Isles would be more southerly and the Gulf Stream would pass far to the north leaving a climate that was far less equable.

Geostrophic Wind

Flow above about 500 m is unaffected by friction with the surface allowing a fine balance to develop between Coriolis and pressure gradient forces so that flow is more or less parallel to the isobars at and above that level. This is known as the geostrophic wind.

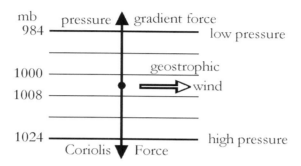

Friction

Air within about 500 m of the surface is affected by friction, which prevents the development of the balanced geostrophic flow seen at higher levels. Friction acts in the opposite direction to airflow so that the air is pulled (or backed) closer to the line of the pressure gradient force.

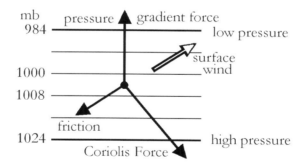

Over land airflow is backed 25-35° from the geostrophic wind direction with the amount varying with the ruggedness of the terrain. That falls to 10-20° over water where there is less friction between air and water. This backing explains why wind arrows on maps cross isobars at 10-35° depending on the surface. The speed of the surface wind over the sea is about two-thirds that of the geostrophic wind but only about one-third of it over land.

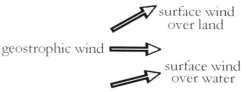

Albacore and Mirror dinghies waiting for the 'off' – Thorpe Bay, Essex

Chapter Six

Local Winds

Most parts of the world experience winds other than those directly associated with the global pressure and wind belts. Regional winds like the Asiatic Monsoon can affect whole continents although most affect a more restricted region such as the eastern part of the Mediterranean. At a local scale, there are winds that affect a particular range of hills or a specific coastal area.

Land and Sea Breezes

In those regions favouring their development, land and sea breezes affect inshore waters and their coastal margins perhaps as far as 100 miles inland. Not all coastlines are affected by such flows with some of the key factors being regional pressure gradients, land and sea surface temperature contrasts and the configuration and topography of a coastline.

Sea Breeze

Under the clear skies of a summer anticyclone, the land temperature rises rapidly while that of adjacent coastal waters rises slowly. The air warmed over the land expands and ascends producing pressure that is locally lower than that over the adjacent sea. As a result, during the late morning the air begins to flow as a sea breeze from high pressure over the sea to the lower pressure over the land.

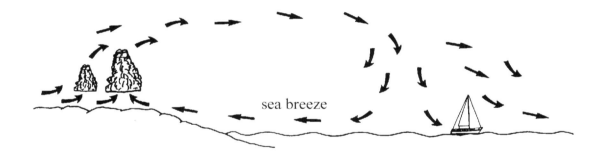

sea breeze

This flow reaches its peak intensity by mid-afternoon when temperatures and therefore the horizontal pressure gradient reach their maximum. The breeze is usually about 7-10 kt but can reach 15-20 kt as the source of the wind moves some 5-10 miles offshore during the afternoon. By that time, the effect of the Coriolis Force has turned the breeze to the right of its earlier heading so that a southerly breeze affecting the south coast of England veers to the south-west or west.

Land Breeze

At night, conditions reverse under clear skies with the land cooling rapidly while the sea retains its heat for longer. High pressure develops over the land giving rise to a land breeze flowing out over the shoreline to the relatively lower pressure offshore. This local pressure gradient is weaker than that which developed during the day so the resulting flow is generally lighter than the sea breeze although it can reach 10-15 kt and 5-10 miles offshore before dying out at dawn.

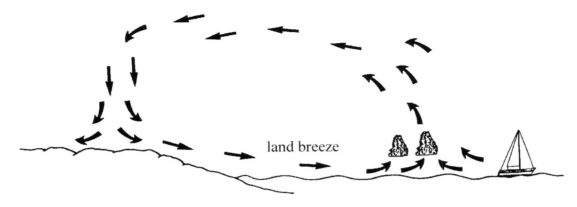

> ### *British Isles*

In the British Isles, land and sea breezes are significant in early summer when a strong breeze can flow from the sea to the shore during the day and then reverse at night. Although they can develop along all coastlines they are most significant along North Sea and English Channel coasts.

These winds are most likely to occur when the islands are dominated by quiet anticyclonic weather with a weak pressure gradient wind. Driven by the land-sea temperature gradient they are most likely to develop in May and June when that gradient is at its maximum. If the pressure gradient wind is in excess of 10 mph as it usually is when frontal systems are passing through, neither breeze develops.

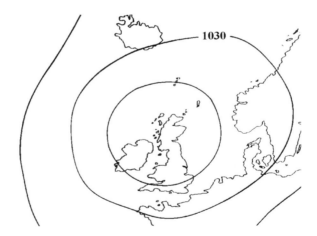

Mountain and Valley Winds

During periods of settled anticyclonic weather with weak regional pressure gradients, locally important up-valley (anabatic) and down-valley (katabatic) flows can develop in areas of high ground especially where an area is crossed by deep valleys.

Anabatic Flows

Under a summer anticyclone, dawn often brings relatively calm conditions with fog hovering over a valley floor. The rising sun heats the upper valley sides creating temperature and pressure gradients between the upper slopes and the initially cooler valley floors. In the late morning, air begins to flow upslope from the locally higher pressure of the valley floor towards ridge crests and summits. The thermals rising above such areas can produce cumulus and possibly shower activity in the afternoon. The thermals are much sought after by soaring birds and glider pilots who travel many miles carried by these currents.

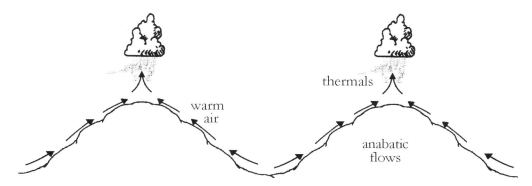

Katabatic Flows

At night conditions are reversed so that a weak pressure gradient encourages cooled air to flow downslope until the valley floor is reached where it turns to follow the valley axis towards surrounding lower ground. This cold air drainage can encourage the development of fog and (in winter) frost in the valley floor while upper slopes face into clear skies.

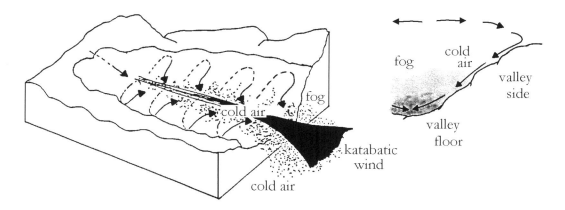

Föhn

Föhn is a generic term used to describe a dry, gusty and relatively warm wind affecting the leeside of a topographical feature. The key aspect of the föhn is that it is formed by air cooling as it passes over an area of highland and then descending the leeside where it warms more quickly than it had previously cooled. The result is locally higher temperatures and lower humidity than on the windward side so that the mass of cloud passing over the highland begins to dissipate giving rise to clearer skies. When a föhn begins, the temperature can rise by several degrees in little more than ten to fifteen minutes.

> ### *British Isles*

In the British Isles, föhn can be recognised in a number of locations. When a southerly wind flows across the Cambrian Mountains in Wales it forms much cloud and gives rise to significant rainfall. However, on descending towards the coast of north Wales it quickly dries and warms giving rise to a localised föhn. Similar effects are experienced on the eastern side of the Pennines in northern England and to the east of the Grampians in Scotland with the occurrence of a föhn being responsible for the exceptionally mild period towards the end of February 2012 in those areas.

Standing Waves

In certain circumstances air flowing across an elongated upland area will descend the leeward side and then rise once more to initiate a series of waves with alternating ridges and troughs. The position of these features remains relatively constant with the position of successive ridges often marked by equally stationary lenticular clouds. A locally reversed flow (rotor) can develop in the immediate lee of the higher ground.

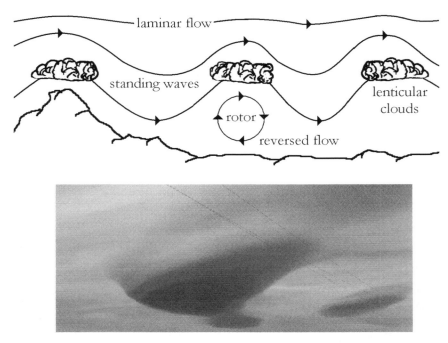

lenticular clouds formed in standing waves

Part B

Weather Systems

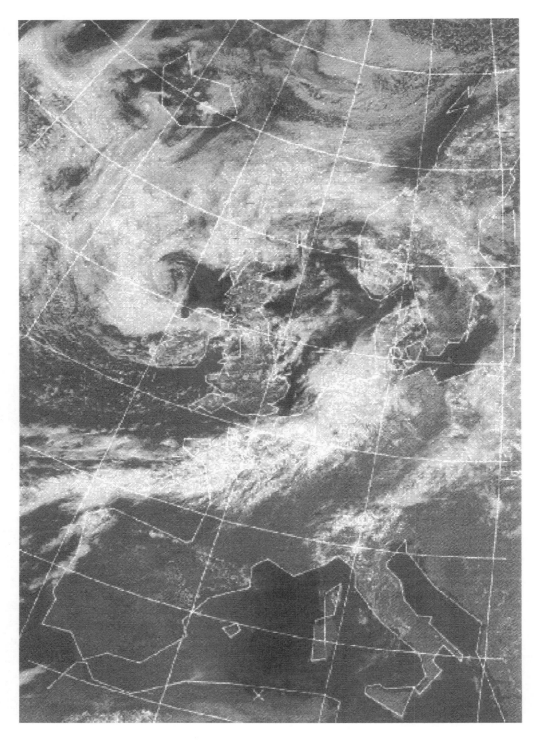

visible satellite image of frontal systems
low pressure centre is to the north-west of Ireland

Part B

Weather Systems

Part B develops the fundamental ideas outlined in the first part of the book so that the reader can begin to understand the day-to-day weather of these islands. Chapter Seven explains in some detail the origin and development of depressions along the polar front. It explains how on occasion the process forms nothing more than a stable wave running along the front while at other times massive systems with gale force winds develop.

Depressions are arguably the key feature of our island weather, which is why their associated weather is described in detail in Chapter Eight with a detailed look at the different types of front. The next chapter considers the nature of thunderstorms, which are occasionally associated with depressions but can develop in a number of other situations.

Chapter Ten looks at air masses, which although not weather systems in the true sense of the word are included here because they are integral to depressions, troughs, anticyclones and ridges. Understanding the nature of air masses helps meteorologists to predict more accurately the weather associated with various systems. The final chapter in this part of the book is a study of anticyclones which although popularly associated with clear skies are far more complicated with many instances of high pressure resulting in what is commonly known as 'anticyclonic gloom'.

clear skies under anticyclone affecting much of western and northern Europe

Chapter Seven

Mid-Latitude Depressions

A mid-latitude depression (mid-latitude cyclone) is a massive multi-dimensional whirl of air dominated by an inward and upward anticlockwise spiral. On a weather map, the key features are a central area of low pressure indicated by an enclosed isobar and frontal zones separating cold and warm air masses. The dominant weather of the typical depression is moderate to strong winds, heavy cloud cover and widespread rain.

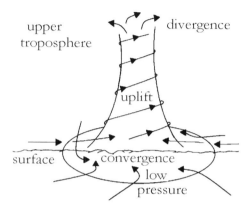

> ### *British Isles*

It is the frequent passage of frontal systems across the British Isles that is responsible for much of the constantly changing weather of the region. It is no coincidence that fine summers including those of 1976 and 1989 occur when changes in the upper atmosphere push depression tracks to the north of these islands. Wet and windy summers like that of 2012 occur when depression tracks are further south. Scotland experienced a wet summer in 2015 because the upper westerly flow including the jet stream with its attendant surface features was further south than normal.

The amount of rain and the strength of the wind associated with any one system is determined by the intensity of that depression. The steep regional pressure gradients of winter bring greater intensity and therefore depressions that are more likely to develop gale force and occasionally storm force winds.

Formation

The origin of any single depression is highly complex involving three-dimensional flows at all altitudes with complex interactions that vary from system to system. The systems affecting the British Isles and north-west Europe all originate in association with the polar front lying above the North Atlantic.

Polar Front

The polar front is an area of significant temperature contrast between polar and tropical air masses meeting in the lower atmosphere over the Atlantic Ocean. When the temperature gradient between these air masses strengthens that area is marked by the North Atlantic Polar Front, which although variable in position is often located over the north-west Atlantic off the eastern seaboard of North America.

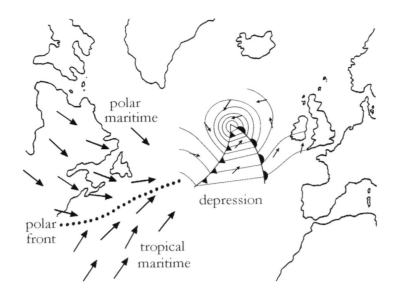

The formation of a mid-latitude depression is related to zones of accelerated and divergent flow within massive troughs in the westerly flow of the upper atmosphere. When the movement of an upper trough across the polar front coincides with a significant temperature gradient across the frontal zone in the lower atmosphere, air is drawn upwards into that trough. The upper air in effect feeds on the energy generated by the temperature contrasts in the lower atmosphere.

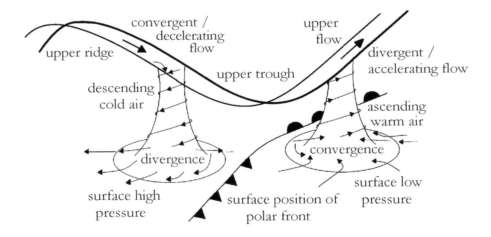

Stable Wave

Initially it is the less dense warm air that is drawn northwards to spiral upwards and over colder air to the north of the front. This rising warm air is replaced at the surface by cold air spiralling downwards and southward into the rear of the developing disturbance.

The opposed but intertwined movements of the warm and cold air quickly distort the polar front forming a small wave with embryonic warm and cold fronts separating the two air masses. Once the wave is formed, the flow in the upper atmosphere drives it in a generally easterly direction across the

Atlantic towards Europe at perhaps 15-20 ms (33-45 mph). Sometimes such waves do not develop into mature depressions but simply move along the polar front across the Atlantic as a stable wave travelling perhaps 1000 km each day with little effect on the weather or the position of the polar front.

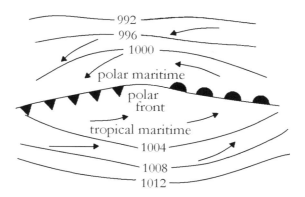

Warm Sector Depression

On those occasions where a system develops beyond a stable wave, the uplift of air continues to such an extent that surface pressure falls sufficiently to cause a pronounced distortion of the polar front. The front is now so distorted that there are in effect two frontal zones with the leading edge (half-moon symbols) separating warmer air from the south driving over colder air to the north while to the west a second edge separates cold air flowing southward from the rising warm air, which it replaces. In an unstable wave, the leading edge will develop into a warm front and the rear edge into a cold front.

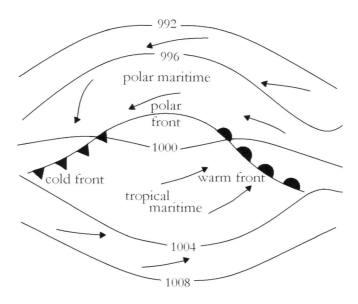

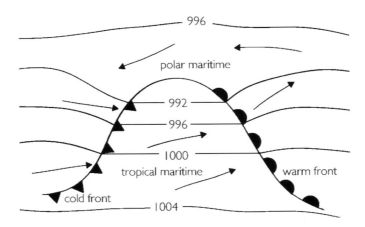

During the first twenty-four hours of an unstable wave, pressure continues to fall rapidly and the fronts become more marked as more air is drawn into the circulation. Beyond twenty-four hours the pressure especially near the apex of the wave has fallen so far that the centre of low pressure is marked by an enclosed isobar the presence of which confirms an easterly flow to the north of the centre and therefore pure cyclonic (ie anticlockwise) circulation.

Coinciding with the establishment of full cyclonic circulation, the amplitude of the wave has increased allowing the full development of a warm sector between the fronts. This is now a mature depression moving east or north-east roughly parallel to the isobars in the warm sector at speeds up to 20 ms (45 mph). Depressions arriving on the shores of the British Isles have invariably reached at least this stage and many will have begun the process of occlusion.

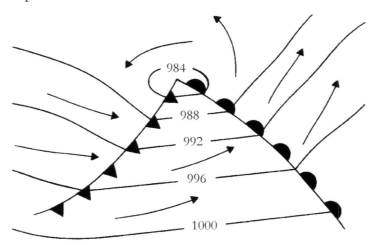

Occlusion

The cold air flowing into the system behind the cold front is moving so much faster than the warm air in the warm sector that it drives the cold front forward at 18-22 ms (40-50 mph) relative to the system as a whole. The relatively gentle slope of the warm front means that more of its surface is in contact with the ground causing friction to reduce its forward velocity relative to the system to perhaps 9-13 ms

(20-30 mph). Inevitably the warm front is caught by the cold front within a matter of hours and the warm sector is gradually lifted off the ground. Beginning at the apex of the system this process works outwards, which is usually southward, so that an increasing length of cold front and warm front is combined into a single occluded front.

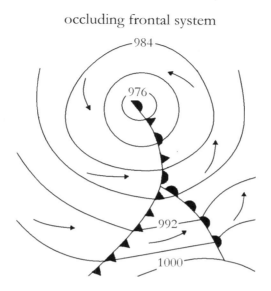

occluding frontal system

Secondary Depressions

It is common to see a weather map showing complex frontal systems with the characteristic feature being the development of a secondary depression on the trailing cold front of the primary depression. This begins with a wave disturbance on that front initiating the development of a secondary centre of low pressure with a circulation similar to that of the primary depression. As the latter weakens, the secondary depression becomes the dominant feature and eventually might be part of a family of four to seven depressions extending across the Atlantic. The warm front of a primary depression is far less likely to develop such secondary features.

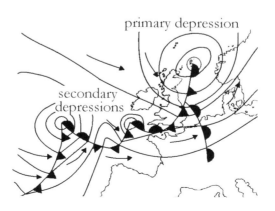

Trough

A trough is an elongated area of low pressure extending outwards from a centre of low pressure into an area of generally higher pressure. These are frequently frontal so that a trough shape can be seen extending along the line of a front as in the first diagram below. Even if it were non-frontal, a trough would bring a mixture of wind, cloud and rain.

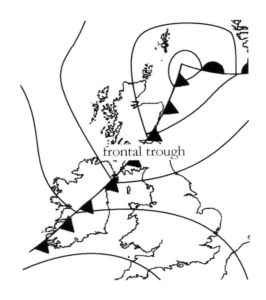

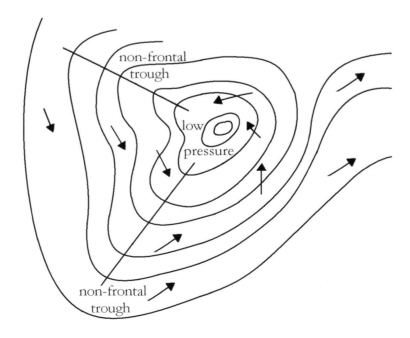

Chapter Eight

Depression Weather

The easiest way to understand and forecast the weather associated with different parts of a depression is to memorise a couple of key diagrams. An observer in the path of a system can expect to experience all the weather changes illustrated in the diagrams. It is important to note that no two depressions are identical and that the speed of movement of the system and the strength of the local wind at different times will vary according to the central pressure, the local pressure gradient and the smoothness of the underlying topography. The amount of rain is proportional in part to the vertical pressure gradient in different areas of a depression so that a system with relatively gentle gradients has weakened uplift along the fronts and therefore less intense precipitation.

It is important to note that on a weather map a front is a single line marking the ground position of the front. In the atmosphere, this line slopes upwards and, in the case of the warm front, downwind of the ground position along a gradient ranging from 1:50 to 1:400 with the average being about 1:150. The warm front moves at a speed equal to approximately two-thirds the strength of the geostrophic wind that is flowing roughly perpendicular towards and in the same direction as the front.

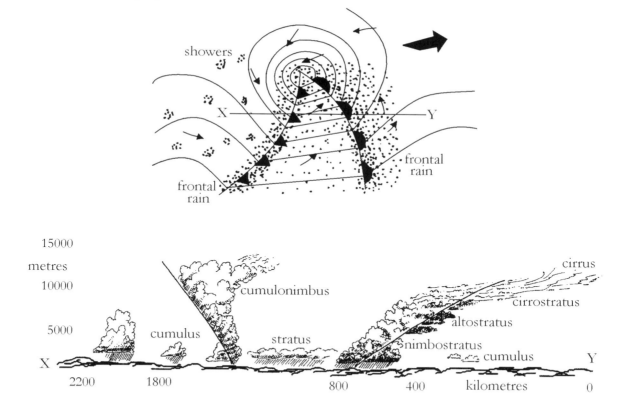

Early Stages

The warm front separates warm air rising above the mass of cold air flowing in a northerly or north-westerly direction ahead of the depression. As the front approaches an observer located directly in its path the weather changes from the west. Initially the sky some hours ahead of a depression is either relatively clear with fragments of cloud or perhaps one-quarter to one-half occupied by isolated shallow cumulus. These 'fair-weather' cumulus are likely to be associated with good visibility and light winds.

The first significant change seen by an observer is cirrus approaching from the north-west followed over the next few hours by progressively lower clouds from an increasingly backed direction (changing from north-west through west to south-west). Given that when the cirrus are first seen the ground position of the front is perhaps 12-24 hours away, if the observer witnessing their approach is on the North Sea coast of England the surface position of the warm front will only have just crossed the west coast of Ireland.

'Fair-weather' cumulus above the observer gradually disappear as sheets of cirrostratus approaching from the west block the sun and dampen the thermal sources driving the cumulus. The sky becomes progressively overcast and the temperature falls as the sun disappears beneath a deepening mass of cloud. The pressure falls quite slowly at this stage while the wind slowly strengthens from a southerly direction with a tendency to back.

Warm Front

Some six to eight hours before the arrival of the warm front, initially intermittent light rain falling from altocumulus becomes continuous and increases in intensity from dark masses of nimbostratus. In these conditions visibility decreases to moderate and occasionally poor.

Warm Sector

When the ground position of the warm front passes over an observer, the cloud base lifts slightly to reveal a low amorphous mass of stratus as the heavy continuous rain gives way to drizzle although in some situations precipitation stops completely. Short-lived squally conditions sometimes accompany the passage of a warm front although the wind quickly falls away to a more moderate breeze veering to the south-west or west. Within the warm sector pressure either continues to fall albeit more slowly or rises slowly or is unchanging.

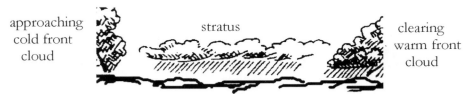

approaching cold front cloud — stratus — clearing warm front cloud

The weather in the warm sector varies according to the precise nature of the air mass in that part of a particular depression but the tropical maritime air is typically 'muggy' with low cloud and drizzle, which is often persistent and widespread. In these conditions, mist is common and visibility often very poor.

Cold Front

The cold front rises upwards and back on itself along a gradient ranging from 1:30 to 1:400 with the average being about 1:70. It moves at a speed approximately equal to the geostrophic wind flowing roughly perpendicular to the front.

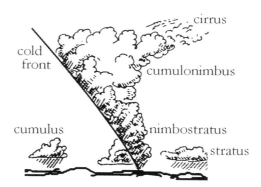

The approach of the cold front is heralded by falling temperatures and a build-up of nimbostratus and cumulonimbus on the western horizon. These are not immediately apparent to a distant observer if they are obscured by a mass of cirrus on their leading edge. The arrival of the ground position of the front is dominated by thick masses of cloud producing perhaps one to two hours of intense rain often accompanied by showers of hail and intense squalls. Very occasionally, such is the vigour of the uplift that it gives rise to thunder and lighting. The temperature inevitably continues to fall under these clouds and the wind veers slightly to the west.

As the front clears away to the east, the sky in the opposite direction brightens as the great mass of frontal cloud breaks-up into distinct clusters. The rains clears with the breaking clouds and at much the same time, the wind veers sharply to the west or north-west and rapidly increases in strength.

Behind the Cold Front

In the polar maritime air behind the cold front, a steady increase in pressure is accompanied by a squally wind often with very strong gusts. Cumulus covering one-half to two-thirds of the sky produce brief but heavy showers invariably accompanied by gusts and on occasion substantial squalls. Thunder, lightning and hail are occasionally experienced at this stage, temperatures fall very rapidly and visibility is very good and sometimes outstanding except in showers when it falls dramatically.

When a clearing cold front is quickly followed by another depression the unstable environment with cumulus and showers is short-lived and cirrus soon appear to the north-west leading to a repeat of the depression weather sequence. However if a ridge builds behind the front, isolated cumulus with limited shower activity are likely to occupy the sky.

Occlusion Weather

The weather associated with an occlusion is inevitably similar to that of a depression. However, the warm front weather is immediately followed by polar maritime conditions because the warm sector (tropical maritime) does not reach down to the surface. There is therefore no true break in the frontal rain, which lasts longer than that associated with a warm front. This frontal rain gives way to a mixture of showers and more continuous spells of rain.

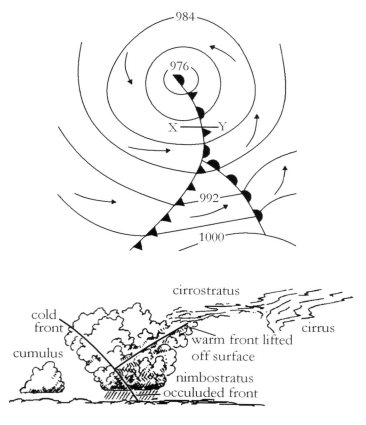

weather sequence along X - Y

Chapter Nine

Thunderstorms

Thunderstorms provide some of the most spectacular weather phenomenon seen in any part of the world. The key characteristics are vivid displays of lightning and violent thunderclaps set against stunning skyscapes dominated by towering cumuliform clouds. These storms are often accompanied by intense rainfall, showers of hail and violent squalls.

> ➢ *British Isles*

Thunderstorms are relatively rare in the British Isles although some storms are seemingly so violent compared with the generally quiet nature of much of the weather of the region that they leave a lasting impression. In most years, eastern England including the east Midlands experiences the largest number of thundery outbreaks with an average of little more than ten a year although on occasion it has risen to twenty or twenty-five. In the south-west, the figure falls to six to ten while in parts of the Lake District and the Isle of Man, it is just two or three. Most of Wales, Scotland and Ireland average eight or nine events each year.

Microcell Thunderstorm

A thunderstorm is rarely generated by a single isolated cumuliform cloud but rather by a group of cloud cells, as is the case with a microcell storm. This consists of a number of cells (clouds) each perhaps one to five kilometres in diameter and lasting for fifty to sixty minutes during which time, it produces lightning for fifteen to twenty minutes.

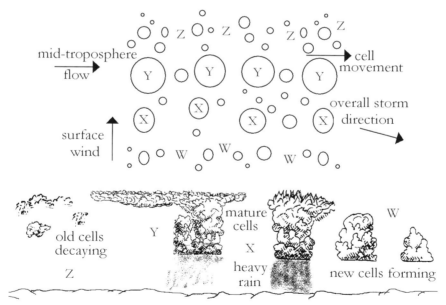

It is because each cell is at a different stage of its life cycle that such storms can last for ten or twelve hours with the cells continually replaced as they die until the trigger mechanism is finally removed. Large violent thunderstorms dominated by a single cell are known as supercell thunderstorms.

Lightning

A discharge of static electricity occurs as charges of opposite sign become concentrated in different parts of a cloud, on the surface below that cloud and within the surrounding air. This build-up of charge generates a gradient of electrical polarity between the cloud and surface and within the cloud until a critical point is reached and electricity is discharged as lightning. The discharge can take place between cloud and surface, between different parts of a single cloud or between two clouds or very occasionally from cloud to the surrounding air. Lightning is usually observed some fifteen to twenty minutes before the onset of precipitation.

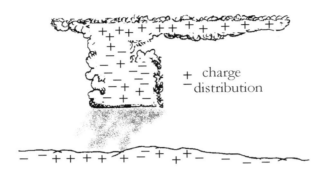

The casual observer of an individual storm can distinguish between fork and sheet lightning although they are identical in origin. While fork lightning shows the actual path of a flash, sheet lightning is what is observed when the path is hidden by clouds so that it appears as a diffuse glow. When fork lightning is observed it is most likely to be from cloud to ground whereas sheet lightning is usually cloud to cloud

> ### *British Isles*

Over the British Isles, about 40% of discharges are cloud to surface with the annual strike rate being about one flash per km^2 of surface every year. Mid-June 2009 was an example of what can occur at any time with thundery showers in many parts of the islands. There were dramatic displays of lightning over the Houses of Parliament in London during the late-afternoon and early evening of June 15th and in East Lothian, sixteen cows taking refuge under a tree were electrocuted.

Thunder

The sudden and intense heating of air along the path of a flash produces a pressure wave equal to ten to one hundred times the normal atmospheric pressure moving outwards at the speed of sound. The characteristic rumbling sound occurs because of the varied times required for the sound to reach an observer from the different parts of a flash which can be two miles long.

The distance of a storm from an observer can be determined quite accurately by recording the time lag in seconds between flash and thunder and dividing that by three to give the distance in kilometres. Thunder can be heard twenty-five to forty kilometres from its source.

> ➤ ***British Isles***

Many thunderstorms in the British Isles occur when irregular heating of the surface creates thermal sources that drive the formation of towering cumuliform clouds. Although this is most commonly associated with high daytime temperatures in eastern and south-eastern England, it is also a feature of winter particularly in northern coastal districts when arctic or polar maritime air is heated from below during its passage to the islands. Storms occur irregularly throughout the year in highland areas when unstable air is forced rapidly upwards by the topography. Another source of thunderstorms is the rapid uplift of warm air immediately ahead of a vigorous cold front.

Squall Lines

When a group of convection cells are aligned perpendicular to the airflow, they form a squall line. In the British Isles, such a linear development of cells is most commonly associated with a cold front crossing the central plains of Ireland and England, especially in summer. The approach of a squall line is heralded by falling temperatures, rising pressure, a strengthening and increasingly squally wind and great masses of towering cumulonimbus.

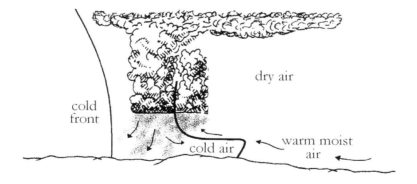

Gusts

Apart from the relatively short-lived intense rainfall, the most obvious characteristic of a squall is the gusty nature of its wind. For observational purposes, the mean wind value is recorded every ten minutes so that the increase from the mean is a gust while a decrease is a lull. A squall is defined as a prolonged gust lasting more than one minute and possessing an increase in speed of at least 16 kt and an overall speed of at least 22 kt. When the wind increases or decreases by at least 10 kt for more than three minutes that speed is recorded as the new mean. The wind will tend to veer (ie change direction in a clockwise sense) in a squall while it tends to back (anticlockwise change) in a lull.

Air moving across a land surface varies constantly in velocity although most of the time that variation is too small to be sensed by the casual observer but is detected by sophisticated equipment. The prime cause of gustiness in stable air is turbulent flow over an irregular surface with the lowest layers of the atmosphere affected more by friction than the air above 500 m. Above that level the air is moving more rapidly and at irregular intervals tends to tumble down to the surface causing a disturbance (gust).

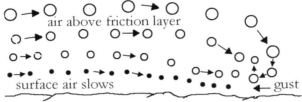

Gusts that are more substantial are usually the result of irregular surface heating producing thermal uplift emphasised by the appearance of cumuliform clouds. Particularly in summer, a clear morning with rising temperature leads to convection and small cumulus associated with light variable winds. When the local thermal environment is sufficiently unstable, the rising air currents producing deeper cumulus and cumulonimbus draw so much air from the surrounding region that they generate significant indraught to the base of a cloud. An observer in the path of these indraughts will feel the sudden and gusty increase in wind strength.

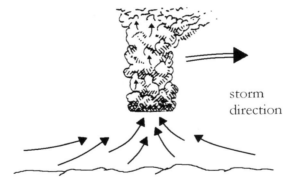

When the condensation process within a cumuliform cloud reaches a critical point, the mass of water drops formed in the cloud begin to descend and exert such a drag on the air that rapid downdraughts gradually overwhelm the previous updraughts. The first rain to fall from a cloud evaporates making the air beneath the base and ahead of the gust noticeably colder (evaporation results in heat loss). This descending and colder air is significantly denser than its immediate surroundings and so forms a highly localised increase in pressure of several millibars. When the downdraughts move beyond the cloud base they hit the surface with considerable force and move outwards in a series of violent gusts in all directions but especially in the direction of cloud movement. These gusts sometimes accompanied by a sudden fall in temperature, extend tens of miles from the cloud base and are veered by as much as 30° from the original wind direction.

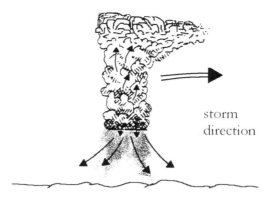

storm
direction

An observer in the path of a squall experiences a series of sudden and sometimes violent gusts arriving in quick succession. Although each lasts for only a minute or so wind strengths are generally 30-50 kt compared to the pre-squall strength of perhaps 5-10 kt and a single gust can be in excess of 60 kt. The most severe squalls are experienced just under or immediately ahead of the arch of the cloud with the squall weakening as it moves away from the parent cloud.

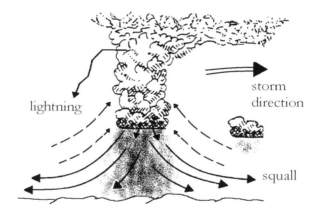

lightning

storm
direction

squall

On water the arrival of a gust is forewarned by 'cat's-paws' on the surface while on land it is presaged by the obvious movement of foliage, dust or litter and a clear sense of air movement felt on the body.

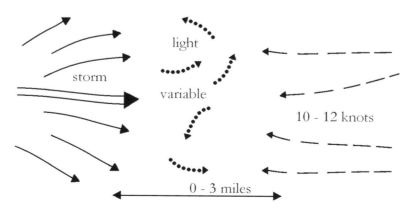

light

storm

variable

10 - 12 knots

0 - 3 miles

In the early stages of a squall, the arrival of strong gusts and the onset of rain roughly coincide but as the cold air spreads away from the cloud it is no longer accompanied by the rain. The finite supply of cold air and descending drops in the cloud gives an average life-span for the squall and showers of only 10-20 minutes although occasionally they can last for thirty minutes. During this period, the cold downdraughts, strong wind and thick cloud can reduce temperatures by as much as 10 °C and visibility is very poor.

cumulonimbus capillatus
note the striated upper parts produced by the mass of water drops turning into snow flakes
– a process known as glaciation

Chapter Ten

Air Masses

Air remaining stationary for weeks at a time above certain parts of the Earth's surface takes on the temperature and humidity characteristics of the surface producing distinct air masses. Air masses are defined by their moisture and thermal characteristics so that an air mass originating over an ocean is maritime (m) whereas one originating over land is continental (c). The thermal characteristics derive from the latitudinal origin of the air so that a distinction can be made between arctic (A), polar (P) and tropical (T). These air masses eventually move vast distances with the result that their characteristics are modified by the surface over which they pass.

Air masses arriving in the British Isles from an arctic or polar source are relatively cold whereas those from a tropical source are warm. Air from the continent has much lower humidity than that arriving from the Atlantic. The main source regions for the British Isles are the north west Atlantic (Pm), the Arctic Ocean (Am), central Europe (Pc), southern Europe-North Africa (Tc) and the Azores (Tm).

Located hundreds if not thousands of kilometres from permanent source regions the British Isles rarely experience prolonged extremes of weather because the area is crossed by substantially modified air and is at the crossroads of such flows. Air travelling towards the region from arctic or polar sources is warmed from underneath becoming unstable and so produces convective clouds. In addition, evaporation from the surface increases its humidity encouraging the development of showers. By contrast air arriving from the tropical ocean to the south-west has been cooled from underneath as it travels poleward across the North Atlantic. In this case, the initially unstable air gradually becomes stable and condensation produces stratiform clouds. Continental air masses arriving from the east undergo less modification as they have experienced only a small change of latitude and have crossed a smaller body of water (the North Sea).

Air Masses in Summer

The British Isles is dominated by westerly air masses in summer with the balance between Pm and Tm going some way to deciding the general nature of a particular summer. Am and Pc are relatively rare at this time of the year.

Polar Maritime (Pm)

Polar maritime air originating over the far north-west of the Atlantic or the northern part of North America is directed into a west or north-west flow between low pressure over Iceland and the Azores high pressure cell.

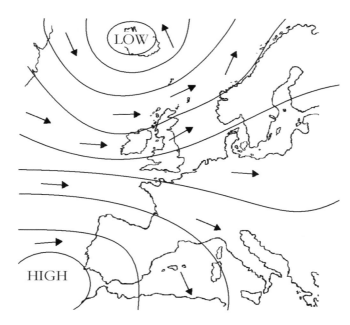

In summer the difference between sea surface temperature and that of the air flowing south-east across the North Atlantic is relatively small. This weakens the convective trigger so that over the open ocean and along windward coasts in the north and west of the British Isles cumuliform development is limited. However, this north-westerly flow brings seasonally low temperatures and squally winds accompanied by light showers to coasts facing north or north-west.

Daytime temperatures are little more than 12-15 °C but inland they are substantially higher giving rise to stronger convection and deeper cumulus producing convective showers that are more frequent, less scattered and likely to be heavier than those on the coast. In particularly unstable air, these showers may well be accompanied by thunderstorms. Inland nights are clear and relatively cool. A prolonged north-westerly flow in summer can spread showers southward over much of the British Isles.

Arctic Maritime (Am)

Arctic maritime air originating over the far north of the Atlantic or from above the Arctic Ocean flows southward between high pressure in the central Atlantic and low pressure over northern Europe / southern Scandinavia. This north or north-easterly airflow is rare in summer.

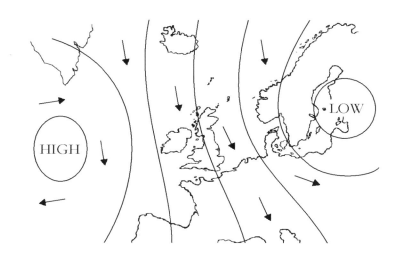

The weather brought by Am is similar to Pm but having travelled a significantly shorter distance from polar latitudes is very much cooler and makes for very disappointing summer days. Northern and north-eastern coasts of England and Scotland are particularly affected by squally showers associated with towering cumulus borne by northerly winds that bring unseasonably cool conditions.

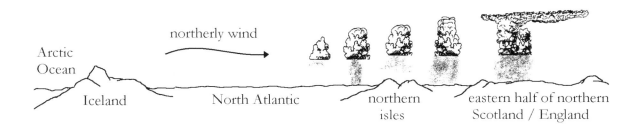

Tropical Maritime (Tm)

Tropical maritime air invariably flows south-west to north-east across the British Isles from a sub-tropical part of the Atlantic lying between the Azores and Bermuda. This high pressure often extends over the western part of the Mediterranean Basin.

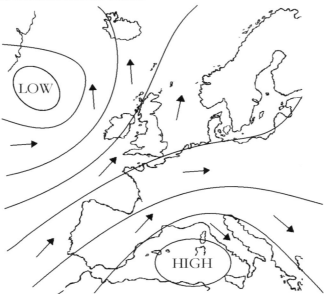

In summer, this air brings warm weather and relatively steady winds to southern and south-western coasts of England, Ireland and Wales. Along these windward coasts low cloud (stratus), advection fog and drizzle are likely. Inland, daytime heating disperses the fog and stratus allowing the formation of shallow 'fair-weather' cumulus that can give rise to the occasional light shower and, if this air is forced over high ground, thunderstorms can develop. Temperatures rise from 18-19 °C along coasts to 20-25 °C inland but under clear skies night temperatures fall sufficiently for the development of radiation fog and dew in inland sheltered areas such as the Somerset Levels.

Leeward coasts tend to be sunnier because the Tm air, having passed over high ground such as the Pennines, warms and dries on its descent causing clouds to dissipate which in part explains the relative dryness of eastern England. Similar situations can be seen in the Welsh Borders as west and south-westerly flows pass over the Cambrian Mountains and descend towards the west Midlands. In Ireland, when the wind is in the west or south-west, the area around Dublin benefits from a similar rainshadow effect.

Polar / Tropical Continental (Pc/Tc)

Polar and tropical continental air masses in summer are very similar with the former having slightly lower temperatures because of its more northerly source. Originating over southern central Europe and very occasionally north Africa both air masses head west or north-west towards the British Isles under the influence of high pressure centred over northern Europe / southern Scandinavia and low pressure over the Mediterranean.

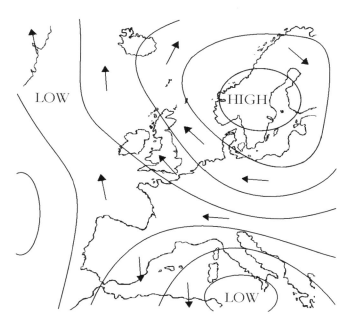

Tropical continental brings rare heatwave conditions to the British Isles especially southern England and the Midlands with daytime temperatures often exceeding 25 °C and occasionally 30 °C. There are long hours of sunshine although visibility can be affected by haze especially if pollution levels are high over the nearby continent. Southern and eastern coasts of England and the eastern coast of Scotland are frequently affected by advection fog locally known as haar or fret that creates significantly cooler conditions compared with a short distance inland. In a slightly stronger wind the fog becomes a thin layer of stratus quickly burnt off by morning sun. Winds are usually light unless a strong sea breeze develops. Night-time temperatures fall to 7-10 °C under clear skies resulting in early morning dew and mist.

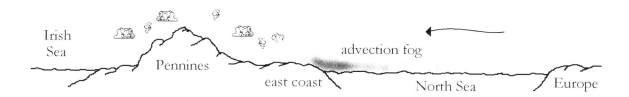

Air Masses in Winter

The winter air masses affecting the British Isles have much the same source regions as summer air masses although Tc is rarely experienced being largely replaced by Pc. Conditions in the atmosphere above each source and along the tracks are invariably quite different to those of summer especially with regard to temperature. The result is that each air mass tends to produce weather that has similarities with summer conditions yet shows obvious seasonal variation.

Polar Maritime

In winter, there is intense convection within this north-westerly airflow because a strong convective trigger is created by the steep temperature gradient between the surface of the Atlantic and the lower layers of the atmosphere. As a result over the open ocean and along windward coasts in the north and west of the British Isles polar maritime brings heavy squally showers day and night with the intensity increasing south to north through the region. Temperatures are low with a daytime maximum of 4-5 °C and visibility is good except in showers.

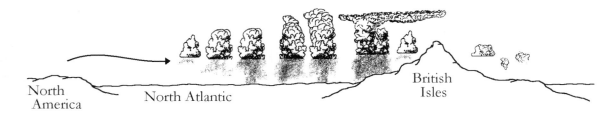

Moving inland the removal of the convective trigger limits shower activity and skies are relatively clear. In such circumstances night-time temperatures are often very low leading to the formation of frost and radiation fog.

Arctic Maritime

Arctic maritime conditions in winter are similar to those that develop in summer with this air mass and are similar to polar maritime in winter but more severe. Intense squally showers, frequently falling as snow, form over the open sea and eastern coasts, especially in Scotland, northern Ireland and northern England. Inland night-time temperatures fall as low as -10 °C and occasionally -20 °C leading to severe frost and dense radiation fog. Daytime maximum temperatures do not rise far above 0 °C and frequently remain below freezing.

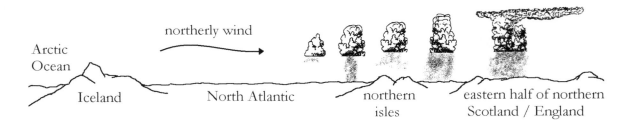

Tropical Maritime

Along south and south-western coasts of England, Ireland and Wales tropical maritime brings advection fog or stratus depending on the wind strength. This is accompanied by poor visibility in the persistent fine drizzle that characterises Tm air over the British Isles. These muggy conditions spread far inland with temperatures rising to 12-15 °C. Following descent from higher ground, the cloud cover is more broken on leeward slopes and marginal plains such as those of the east coast of England and the north coast of Wales.

Polar Continental

Pc brings very low temperatures, biting east winds and heavy snow showers to eastern coasts of England and Scotland with the amount of snowfall often increasing in a southerly direction (the photograph shows a snowy beach on a winter's day in Thorpe Bay, Essex). Showers are unlikely inland although temperatures rarely rise above freezing during the day and at night slip to -10 °C or even -15 °C. Frost and radiation fog are widespread.

Bamburgh Castle (Northumberland) in summer seen through a light coastal mist (fret)

A sunny summer's day in Rutland

Chapter Eleven

Anticyclones

Anticyclones are either permanent or quasi-permanent areas of high pressure either formed as part of the global circulation or as relatively short-lived features embedded in the generally westerly flow of the mid-latitudes. Areas of high pressure are dominated by air that is descending in a clockwise and outward spiral. The descending air expands and warms in a process that is the opposite of that found in the rising spiral associated with a centre of low pressure.

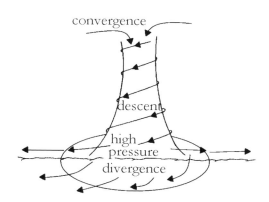

Anticyclones are divided into cold and warm types although their complex differences are beyond the scope of this text. Suffice to say that a cold anticyclone tends to form above a cold surface such as Siberia in winter. Above the surface, the temperature increases with altitude as the cold surface is left behind allowing an inversion to form at the base of air subsiding from the upper troposphere.

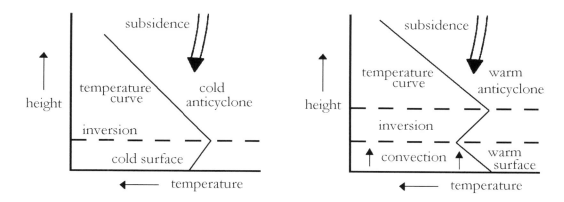

Warm anticyclones tend to be associated with a warm surface so that convection dominates the lowest layers causing air temperatures to fall until an inversion is reached relatively close to the surface. The terms cold and warm can be misleading when applied to anticyclones as evidenced by the Azores high, which structurally is a cold anticyclone situated above a warm surface. In both types, the inversion is likely to be found at an altitude of 1.5-6 miles coinciding with the base of the descending air.

Anticyclonic Weather

Descending air is particularly concentrated between 1.5-6 km above the surface where it becomes more stable and falling humidity tends to bring clear skies. However, a specific high pressure system can bring cloud and wind depending on atmospheric conditions above the surface and the position of an observer relative to the centre of the system.

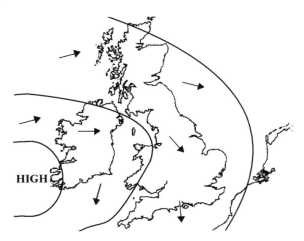

Widely spaced isobars confirm the weak pressure gradients producing light winds flowing gently outwards from the centre. The direction and strength of the wind affecting any one location depends on distance and direction from the anticyclonic centre. The air rotating in a clockwise direction around the centre increases in strength away from the centre while moving in a less anticyclonic manner. The pressure gradient steepens and induces stronger winds towards the edge of an anticyclone especially if a frontal system is approaching.

The precise weather experienced during an anticyclone depends on the position of its centre. If an anticyclone develops above the English Midlands, there is a possibility of clear skies with the weather varying according to the season. However, when an inversion develops close to the surface and the circulation draws in maritime air the weather is more likely to be that typified by anticyclonic gloom.

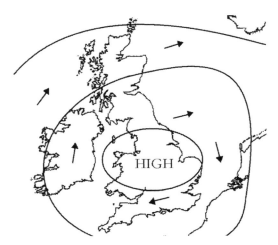

When the pressure centre is offset the region is affected by marginal air masses circulating around the system. The weather, which is unlikely to be typical of an anticyclone, would be dominated by the nature of the air mass affecting a particular location. When, for example, high pressure is centred to the west of Ireland the eastern side of the British Isles in particular is affected by cool showery arctic maritime air.

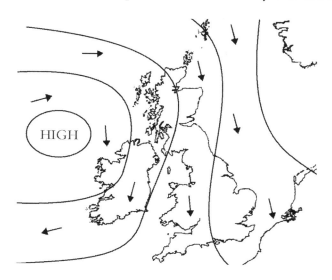

Winter Weather

Clear anticyclonic skies lead to very cold conditions day and night as temperatures fall to below -10 °C encouraging hard frosts that persist through the short days when temperatures often fail to rise above 0 °C. Radiation fog is likely to be persistent in the low temperatures in part because it is trapped below an inversion.

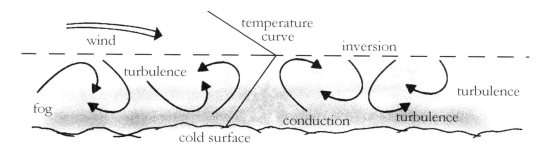

Below an inversion, a moist surface encourages the formation of stratocumulus and stratus, which can persist in the weak winds and low temperatures producing anticyclonic gloom.

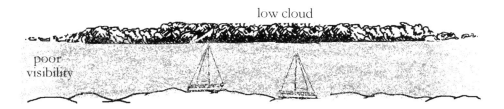

Summer Weather

In summer, clear skies lead to cool nights encouraging the formation of dew and radiation fog before dawn. The fog is especially common along valley floors because of cold air drainage from higher slopes. Soon after sunrise, the fog usually clears quickly in the rising temperatures although it can linger above valley floors and along coasts. In favourable conditions, cumulus develop during the late morning and by mid-afternoon are likely to be quite deep and if their tops spread below a stable layer the sky is likely to become overcast. Land and sea breezes are typical of anticyclones during early summer.

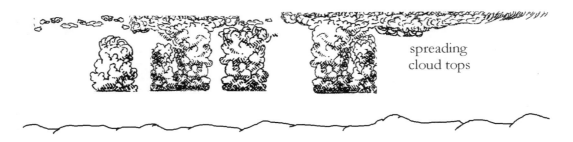

spreading cloud tops

Ridge

A ridge is an elongated area extending away from a centre of high pressure introducing a relatively narrow finger of higher pressure into an area of otherwise lower pressure. Such a ridge often develops between two depressions and affects a location soon after the passage of a cold or occluded front.

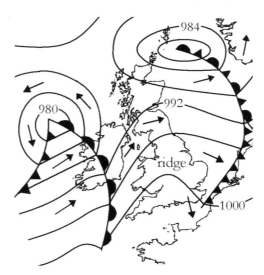

A ridge can develop in other circumstances as for example when a tongue of higher pressure extends northwards from the Azores to cover much of the British Isles.

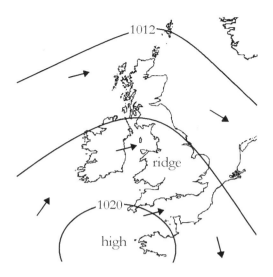

Ridges are typically associated with brief periods of fair weather and light winds and, occurring as they do between depressions and their strong winds, are often referred to as 'windows of opportunity' much favoured by aviators and sailors.

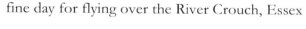

fine day for flying over the River Crouch, Essex

Blocking Anticyclones

When stationary centres of high pressure persist for several days or even longer in the eastern Atlantic or across western and or northern Europe or the Mediterranean, they form a block allowing little or no change in day to day weather. When an anticyclone persists across the average track of depressions, they are forced either to the north or to the south of that track so that their changeable, wet and windy weather is not experienced in the British Isles. These blocking anticyclones tend to occur in favoured geographical locations two of which are discussed below.

Blocking Anticyclone over Scandinavia

When an anticyclone persists over Scandinavia, the polar front is forced far to the south taking with it the depressions that now tend to pass across southern France and possibly into the Mediterranean. The circulation around this high pressure drives an easterly flow across the continent and on towards the British Isles with wind strengths increasing in a southerly direction. It is the tendency to dry easterly winds with this block that produced the severe winter of 1962-3 and the hot dry summer of 1976.

The air over the continent is notably dry because of subsidence within the high and the continental track. Passing over only a relatively narrow body of water (the North Sea) the Pc/Tc air arriving in the British Isles is very dry so that skies tend to be clear although convection over the sea in winter can lead to significant coastal snow showers notably in the south-east, which does not normally experience significant snowfall. In summer heatwave conditions are possible although the east coast often suffers from advection fog, which in this situation can lead to daytime temperatures several degrees lower than locations only a short distance inland.

Blocking Anticyclone west of Ireland

When an anticyclone persists over the North Atlantic to the west of Ireland, the polar front is forced far to the north so that depressions tend to pass across Iceland and on into the far north of the Arctic. The circulation around this high pressure drives a northerly or north-westerly flow across the Atlantic with wind strengths increasing in a northerly direction.

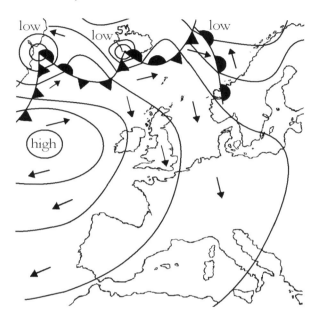

The air arriving in the British Isles is maritime but whether it is polar or tropical varies according to its history. In some situations a location will experience warmer than normal Pm because the air has travelled far to the south before swinging back north around the centre and finally heading for the British Isles. On other occasions the Tm air flows north around the western edge of the high before approaching the islands as a cooler than usual Tm flow.

In either situation, shallow cumulus and or layers of stratocumulus are likely to develop under a low-level inversion. These can produce light showers over the sea and coastal locations in summer but further inland in winter anticyclonic gloom is likely to develop.

fine anticyclonic weather can be ideal for ballooning and sailing

Part C

Weather Forecasting

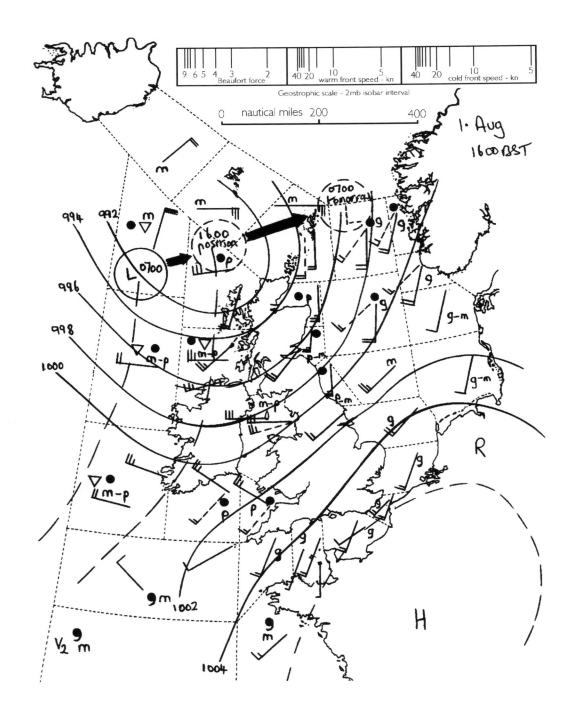

weather reports plotted on a map in preparation for
plotting forecast positions of weather systems (see map, page 82)

Part C

Weather Forecasting

Now that you have a good grounding in the elements that affect the weather of the British Isles, you need to acquire an understanding of professional weather predictions if you wish to create your own forecasts.

Chapter Twelve introduces synoptic charts (surface pressure maps). There are twenty separate examples each of which provides a synoptic chart of the British Isles, a description of the synoptic situation and an analysis of how the weather is likely to develop over the next few hours. Once you have worked your way through these you will have a much better understanding of similar charts found in print and digital media.

Chapter Thirteen takes you a stage further by discussing how you can interpret changes in the sky. This will help you to refine a regional synoptic forecast into one that is appropriate to your location for a specific period.

The final two chapters describe the production and transmission of commercial forecasts through various outlets. Channels, frequencies and times are detailed allowing you to find a suitable forecast for any location in the British Isles at any time of day or night. There is also very useful information about the forecasts available on a number of websites.

The appendices that follow Part C provide information about useful weather based websites, the units used in meteorology, the Beaufort Scale and the symbols used on weather maps. There is also a highly useful glossary.

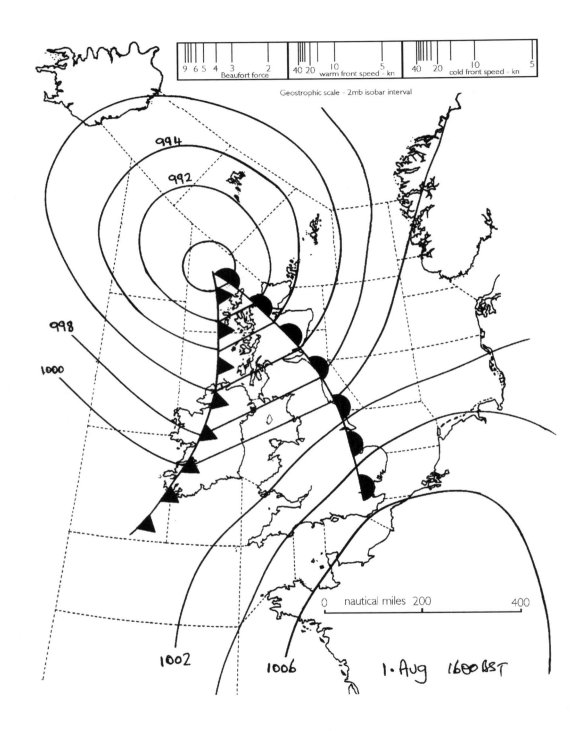

weather systems drawn
using the data plotted on page 80

Chapter Twelve

Surface Pressure Maps

The two factors to consider when first looking at a surface pressure map are whether a frontal system is affecting the area of interest and if so which part of the system will be passing through that area. When a frontal system is not relevant, you need to consider if the location is directly affected by an anticyclone in which case the short-term forecast will possibly be quite simple. Alternatively, airflow (wind direction) might be the dominant factor requiring you to consider air mass characteristics.

Frontal System Forecast

When a frontal system is predicted to dominate the area of interest decide which part (or parts) of the system will pass through at a particular time and compare the situation with the diagram of depression weather (page 53).

So, if the depression is positioned as shown in the map you would expect the weather at X, Y and Z to be as described below. To consider other scenarios simply move the centre of low pressure, warm front and cold front to different locations and reconfigure the forecast.

X

X is probably twelve to fifteen hours ahead of the ground position of the warm front. The pressure is beginning to fall as the pressure gradient slowly steepens driving a slight increase in the hitherto gentle southerly breeze. Some four to six-eighths of the sky are occupied by shallow to medium depth cumulus, which in the past few hours have produced isolated scattered showers. However, the weather is now dry as cirrus approaching at high altitude from the north-west indicates the distant approach of the warm front. The temperature, which had fallen under the influence of the cool Pm airflow, has stopped falling.

Y

At Y, the pressure has steadied after several hours during which weather stations recorded a significant fall. The wind has veered to the south-west, is gentle to moderate and steady in strength. The sky is completely overcast in the Tm flow with low stratus making for a rather muggy period as temperatures have risen significantly since the passage of the warm front. Intermittent drizzle continues to fall.

Z

At Z, the pressure has risen quite rapidly during the past hour. This coincides with a veer in the wind direction from west to north-west. The edge of the great mass of frontal clouds marks a clear line in the sky immediately to the east of the observer. The heavy rain of the past hour has given way to fine weather but the grey stalks of distant showers on the horizon and the falling temperature reflect the arrival of cooler and unstable Pm air.

Anticyclone Forecast

When the area of interest is directly under an area of high pressure the weather is likely to be typical of an anticyclone. In the situation illustrated below with an anticyclone covering the British Isles the air through much of the atmosphere is descending and becoming warmer and drier leading (probably) to clear skies although confusingly (and beyond the scope of this text) some anticyclonic situations lead to the aptly named anticyclonic gloom. The clear skies within an area of high pressure lead to different weather outcomes according to the season with high temperatures in summer and significantly lower temperatures in winter.

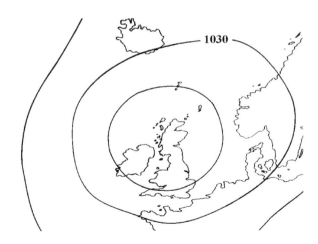

Airflow Direction (Air Masses)

In a situation where an anticyclone is adjacent to but not directly over the British Isles it draws air across the islands from any point of the compass according to the position of the high pressure centre. The same effect would be achieved if the anticyclone rather than being close to the British Isles was hundreds or even thousands of kilometres distant over Scandinavia, Siberia, North Africa, the Arctic Ocean or the Atlantic Ocean.

What you have to do in an air mass situation is determine the source of the air and the route over which it has passed. You can then decide whether it is, for example, Pm or Tc and of course bear in mind the time of year.

In the illustration, the high pressure west of Greenland is driving Pm air across the North Atlantic to the British Isles on a summer day. The weather on northern and western coasts will be cool and breezy with scattered and relatively shallow cumulus producing no more than light showers. As the air continues southward into England the warmer land surface is likely to generate considerable convective uplift producing deep cumulus and cumulonimbus giving rise to heavy showers possibly accompanied by thunder and lightning.

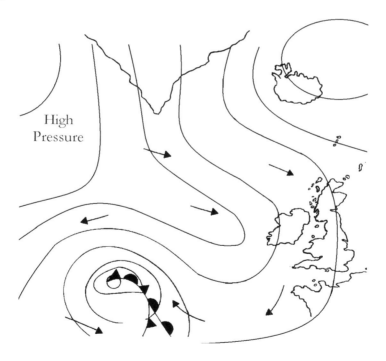

In the following illustration, the Azores high pressure is driving Tm air towards the British Isles in winter. The resulting weather over much of the southern half of the islands will be muggy with either stratus giving rise to widespread drizzle or advection fog. Inland the weather will be much the same except where a föhn effect is experienced as the air descends the leeside of higher ground. Clearer weather can be expected along the north coast of Wales in the lee of the Cambrian Mountains and in parts of eastern England in the lee of the Pennines.

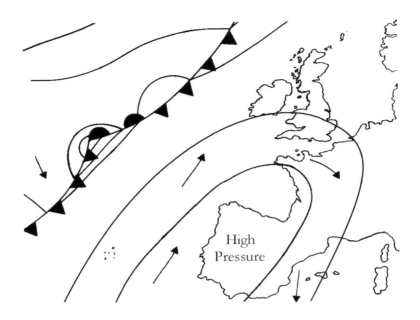

Synoptic Examples

The following pages provide a series of worked examples of synoptic situations. Following each title the season and headline weather are indicated. Although each example focuses on a particular season the synoptic situation and weather forecast may well occur at other times of the year. The headline weather emphasises a particular aspect of the weather to be considered although the situation is likely to give rise to other significant weather. In the first example, the rainy and changeable weather might well be accompanied by strong winds and of course, a depression might follow the described path at any time of the year.

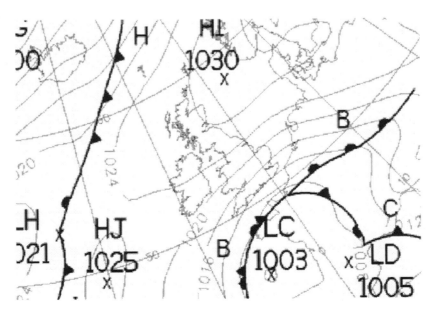

1. Depression tracking west to east across the British Isles

Season: Late autumn
Weather: Rainy and changeable

Synopsis

An area of low pressure (984 mb) is centred 150 km west of the Outer Hebrides and 200 km north of Ireland. This is a mature depression with a warm front extending north-west to south-east close to the Isle of Man and the Welsh Marches. The cold front curving away to the south-west is fast approaching the west coast of Ireland. In this instance, the jet stream is quite sluggish so the fronts will pass relatively slowly west to east across the British Isles during the next twenty-four hours.

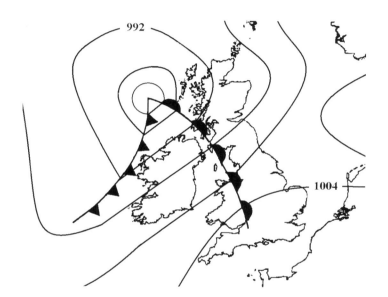

Weather Forecast

Periods of prolonged rainfall separated by showery outbreaks that are lighter and more intermittent will dominate the weather. All locations south of the low centre can expect cloud building from the west to be associated with a sustained period of frontal rain. The passage of that band brings a change to lighter rain or drizzle, which for a time may stop in some locations All areas to the west of the warm front have already experienced this sequence of weather. A brief period of heavy rain from cumuliform clouds possibly associated with thunderstorms will accompany the passage of the cold front across the British Isles.

Locations in the path of the fronts are likely to experience similar changes to places upwind although locations further east will probably receive less rainfall as the cloud cover is likely to be more broken. This is in part because the system will have lost much of its moisture by the time it has reached eastern regions and because of the rainshadow effect. The relatively wide spacing of the isobars suggests that strong winds are unlikely even in exposed locations and gales will definitely not occur.

2. Frontal system crossing the British Isles (autumn)

Season: Autumn, most likely – although can be any season
Weather: Dull

Synopsis

Dull overcast weather often develops with the widespread slow uplift of moist air associated with a low pressure system and fronts are usually involved. The following section considers the possibility of a dull day with reference to three different synoptic situations.

Synopsis One

Weak low pressure (999 mb) is centred over the Isle of Islay. This slow moving system has a warm front extending south-east through the Wash and a cold front aligned north-east to south-west through Ireland.

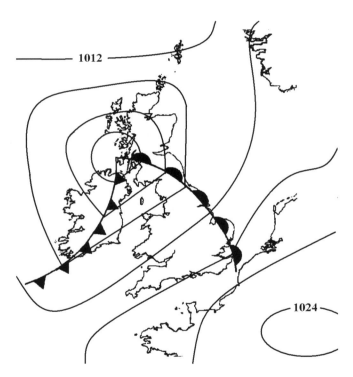

Weather Forecast (south coast of England)

The dominant weather characteristic along the south coast for the next few hours will be low cloud (primarily stratus) with few if any breaks. If there is sufficient frontal uplift the stratus will probably give rise to fine drizzle, which will be thoroughly unpleasant for unprepared walkers. Over high ground such as the Downs the uplift will be more significant with the cloud cloaking the ground in a fine mist (in effect low cloud). Periods of heavy rainfall will occur if layers of altostratus formed in the air above the stratus give rise to drops that coalesce into larger drops as they fall through the lower cloud.

Synopsis Two

The centre of a low pressure (988 mb) system is positioned to the north of the Shetland Islands with a cold front trailing north-east to south-west as it approaches the Western Isles. High pressure (1020 mb) is centred over the English Channel / northern France. Circulation around the two systems combines to produce a south-westerly flow across the British Isles. (this synopsis would also describe a mild day in winter).

Centres of low pressure tend to track far to the north of the British Isles in this way when the jet stream is displaced to a more northerly latitude and takes the polar front with it.

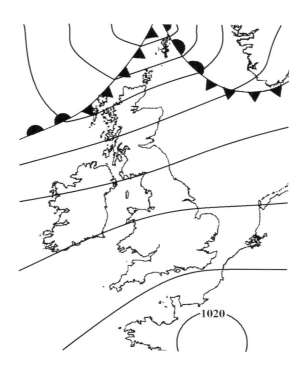

Weather Forecast (Scottish Borders)

The air circulating around the southern edge of the high pressure cell is drawn north-eastwards over a cooling sea producing layers of cloud at low-level. There is limited vertical development of this cloud because of the tendency for air to sink and dry within high pressure, even on the margins of cells. The temperature inversion that forms between this sinking air and that flowing north-eastwards, effectively caps the upward growth of cloud. The result will be extensive sheets of stratocumulus covering the western slopes and summits of the north Pennines, the Cheviots and the Southern Uplands of Scotland. The cloud base will be 500-2000 m so that uplift over high ground produces a thickening of the cloud and possibly light rain or drizzle will ensue. Descent on the leeward side of hills stops the rain and possibly leads to significant breaks in the cloud.

Synopsis Three

A frontal system is approaching the British Isles with its warm front aligned north to south through the centre of Ireland. Ahead of the warm front there is a ridge that can be expected to slide away to the south or south-east. The ridge may have the effect of suppressing the vertical development of any cumuliform clouds forming ahead of the warm front.

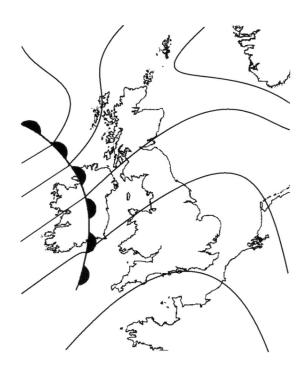

Weather Forecast (western parts of UK)

The defining weather characteristic over Wales and western parts of England and Scotland will be the approach of a succession of cloud types (photos below) from the west. Each will be progressively lower in the sky and darker with the sun gradually obscured as a dense layer of cloud covers the whole sky.

| mix of high cirrus and lower cumulus | mid-level altocumulus | low-level stratus |

3. High pressure over northern Britain

Weather: Dull (anticyclonic gloom)
Season: Winter

Synopsis

The map shows an anticyclone centred over northern Scotland and extending southward across the northern half of the British Isles. The descending anticyclonic spiral of air moves outwards from the centre driving an easterly flow across much of the region.

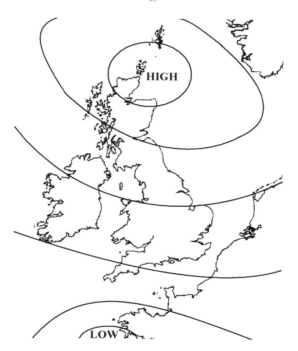

Weather Forecast (England and Wales)

The air passing east to west across the British Isles gains moisture in its passage across the North Sea. Cooling over the land surface causes the relative humidity to increase to the point where low-level clouds form and spread below the temperature inversion typical of high pressure. Once formed the mix of stratus and stratocumulus is likely to persist creating the dull conditions of anticyclonic gloom that will be slow to disperse because of the lack of strong wind. The situation is exacerbated in large towns and cities where pollution is trapped by the inversion. Radiation fog will linger in this situation especially over poorly drained areas such as the Somerset Levels and the Vale of York.

Conditions will only improve when the high pressure weakens and or moves away allowing the arrival of stronger winds from a different direction that draw in drier air allowing relative humidity to fall and so encouraging the dispersal of the clouds.

4. Ridge over eastern England retreating as warm front approaches

Weather: Cloudy
Season: Any
(A cloudy day is defined as one when for most of the daylight period the sky has a cover of at least 5/8 and usually closer to total cover. The light tends to be significantly stronger than that of a dull day because the clouds have a higher base and a broader mix of hues).

Synopsis (same situation as page 90)

A ridge of high pressure extends south to north over the North Sea while a warm front approaching from the west has just crossed the west coast of Ireland. On this occasion, the ridge is predicted to slowly slide away to the south-east allowing the front to cross the British Isles followed inevitably by a cold front.

Weather Forecast (eastern England)

The warm front is far enough to the west to allow the full effect of the ridge to be felt along the eastern half of England. Descending air within the ridge has created a temperature inversion near the surface restricting cloud development to shallow 'fair-weather' cumulus occupying 5-6/8 of the sky. An observer on the east coast of England will see the movement of high altitude clouds through breaks in the cumulus. Arriving from the west, these herald the approach of the warm front as fibrous trails of cirrus are gradually replaced by sheets of cirrostratus followed by altostratus. For a few hours, the observer will see multi-layered clouds with remnants of cumulus drifting at an angle to the high-level clouds creating an overcast but interesting sky.

5. Northerly Airflow

Weather: Cloudy
Season: Winter

Synopsis

A northerly airflow is most likely to be experienced in one of two situations. The first is when a non-frontal low is centred over the north-east part of the North Sea and there is an area of high pressure towards Iceland. The second scenario (shown below) would be in the airflow behind a cold front passing in a southerly or south-easterly direction across the British Isles. (Both scenarios also encourage the development of a showery day in winter).

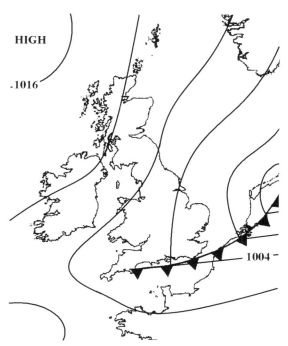

Weather Forecast (coastal districts)

The northerly airflow (Am) is warmed from underneath during its passage southward across the sea. This results in convection driving the formation of large cumulus giving rise to heavy snow showers over the sea. These showery conditions do not penetrate far inland but continue along both west and east coasts sometimes as far south as the Thames Estuary. Snow accumulation can be quite significant and tends to increase in a southerly direction because increased distance from the high pressure centre gives a greater depth to the unstable layer extending from the surface upwards. It can feel bitterly cold with temperatures rising little above freezing.

Coastal locations within these areas will experience total cloud cover with few if any breaks so that sunshine totals are very low. Although cumulus bases are often dark, there is a broad range of hues and sufficient structure in the cumuliform outlines to ensure that the light although rarely good is not as bad as that of a dull day.

6. High pressure centred over the British Isles

Weather: Calm
Season: Any

Synopsis

An area of high pressure (1036 mb) centred over the English Midlands extends from the Atlantic Ocean north-west of Spain, across the British Isles and far into northern and central Europe. The air at the heart of the high pressure is descending from mid and upper levels in a slow, outward and anticyclonic spiral. In the absence of frontal systems, the horizontal pressure gradient is weak indicating that air movement across the region is slow and that the weather will be relatively constant until the high pressure moves away.

Weather Forecast

Winds will be light with extensive areas of calm. However, in summer such conditions often lead to the development of a sea breeze in coastal districts in the late morning in which case the wind might locally be quite strong in the afternoon before fading away towards evening. A sea breeze tends to veer during the day because of the Coriolis effect so that an initially south-easterly breeze along the south coast would gradually become more southerly.

A sea breeze brings cooler conditions to coastal districts and can bring advection fog if the airflow is not too strong.

7. Col centred over the British Isles

Weather: Calm
Season: Any

Synopsis

The situation shown on the map is a relatively common occurrence with a broad area of high pressure forming over central and eastern Europe at the same time as an extension of the Azores high moves towards the British Isles. Neither area of high pressure is directly over the islands or has a direct effect on the weather of the area.

A decaying frontal system is occluding as it passes across southern France into the Mediterranean. An active frontal system is moving rapidly north-east between Iceland and Norway so as to pass to the north-west of the British Isles with little or no effect on the islands. The map shows the British Isles covered by a col characterised by relatively uniform pressure and therefore a very weak horizontal pressure gradient.

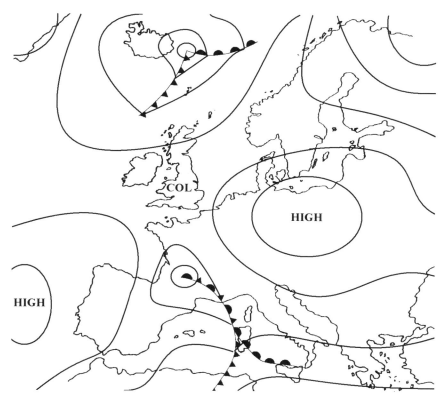

Weather Forecast

Much of the British Isles will be affected by light winds often falling away to an absolute calm. The weather, apart from the wind, will almost certainly be dry, with broken cloud occupying 5-6/8 of the sky although completely overcast conditions are possible if stratocumulus and or altocumulus spread below a low-level inversion.

8. Frontal system decaying over the British Isles

Weather: Overcast
Season: All year round but particularly the second half of the year

Synopsis

The map shows a frontal system in the final stages of decay passing eastward across the British Isles. The warm and cold fronts have almost fully occluded and the low centre has split into two separate centres, which are filling (ie the pressure is rising) and are no longer attached to the fronts. This reflects the significantly decreased temperature gradient across the fronts, which means that the pressure gradient has similarly fallen away. Uplift has slowed considerably so that precipitation is lighter and more intermittent than would be expected with mature warm and cold fronts.

Weather Forecast

An extensive area of cloud albeit with significant breaks will cover much of the British Isles as the remnants of the frontal system pass eastward. Intermittent light rain falling from altocumulus and stratus will affect many areas with a band of heavier and slow moving rain accompanying the occluded front. Relatively light southerly winds ahead of the front will veer to the south-west and briefly strengthen as the front passes through followed by a period of showery weather.

9. High pressure centred over the North Sea

Weather: Dry and sunny over central and southern England
Season: Summer

Synopsis

In high summer, an area of high pressure (1039 mb) is centred over the northern half of the North Sea. The anticyclonic circulation draws a mix of Pc and Tc towards the British Isles from an easterly or south-easterly direction. The pressure gradient outward from the centre of the high is gentle with the air descending in a slow outward spiral.

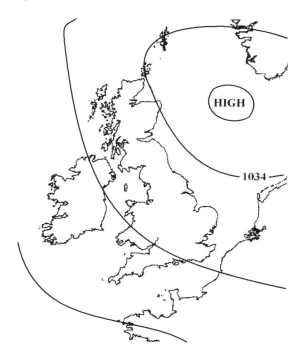

Weather Forecast

The most obvious aspect of the weather in this situation is likely to be clear blue skies. This is the result of air arriving from the south-east having followed a predominantly continental track so that the relative humidity is usually only 10-20%. Although the air is unstable and there is significant near surface turbulence and thermal activity, its inherent dryness prevents the development of cloud.

Daytime temperatures are likely to be high especially in southern and central England although under clear skies temperatures fall away rapidly during the night. This can lead to extensive dew and fog in the early hours although that will clear quickly with the rising sun. Haze may reduce visibility over large towns and cities especially if pollution levels are high over the near continent. On rare occasions, smog will be a factor in London and some south coast towns.

A sea breeze system is likely to develop along eastern and southern coasts and in the early part of summer that may draw advection fog onto those areas so that there is a significant contrast with the weather a few miles inland.

10. High pressure over Scandinavia and northern Europe

Weather: Dry and sunny over central England
Season: Winter

Synopsis

An extensive area of high pressure (1047 mb) has developed across Scandinavia and northern Europe. The anticyclonic circulation draws Pc air in a downward and outward spiral across central Europe and the North Sea towards the British Isles.

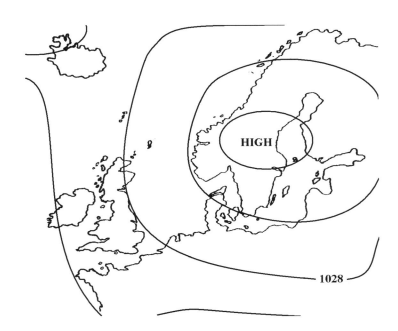

Weather Forecast

The air over northern Europe / Scandinavia is descending in a slow and outward anticyclonic spiral generating an easterly flow across Europe towards the British Isles. The Pc air in its source region is cold, dry and stable below a low-level inversion that increases in altitude in a southerly direction.

The air crossing the North Sea from central/northern Europe gains moisture and is sufficiently warmed by the sea to generate convection producing showers along the east coast of Britain. These showers are more frequent and more intense further south because of the greater depth of unstable air so that snow accumulations are likely to be more significant than in locations further north. However, as soon as the air passes inland the convective trigger and source of moisture is left behind leaving only fragments of cumulus to drift on the wind. The lower atmosphere within the Pc reverts to its normal dry and stable character resulting in clear skies above the English Midlands and other areas beyond the east coast. Snow falling on the ground is likely to linger and accumulate because of the low temperatures day and night accompanied by severe frost and radiation fog.

11. High pressure west of Ireland (winter)

Weather: Dry and sunny over inland parts of southern Britain
Season: Winter

Synopsis

An area of high pressure (1040 mb) has developed to the west of Ireland. The anticyclonic circulation in this situation draws a northerly Am airflow north to south across Britain. The air at the heart of the anticyclone is descending in an outward anticlockwise spiral so at mid and high altitudes it is relatively dry and stable. However, the northerly flow gains moisture from the surface which being relatively warm generates convection beneath a low-level inversion. The latter increases in height away from the centre of the anticyclone so that the depth of unstable air tends to be greater towards the east.

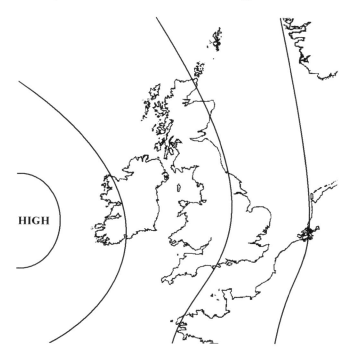

Weather Forecast

The unstable Am air arriving on the north coast of Scotland is bitterly cold and full of snow showers. These will spread far down both east and west coasts although one side is likely to be more affected than the other, according to whether the north wind has an element of east or west in it.

These coastal showers are likely to continue southward as far as the Severn and Thames estuaries. Inland, particularly in southern Scotland and into England and Wales, the lack of a convective trigger inhibits cloud formation so that skies tend to be clear through the day and into the night although fragments of cloud continue to drift southward on the wind.

12. Non-frontal low pressure over southern England

Weather: Thunderstorms
Season: Summer

Synopsis

A non-frontal centre of low pressure has drifted across the English Channel and is continuing on a northerly path into the English Midlands.

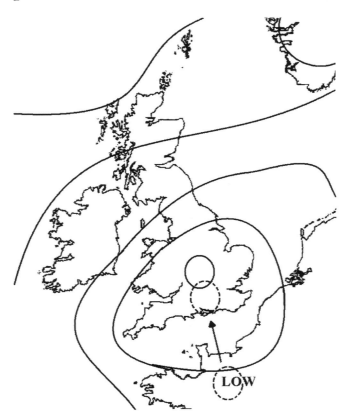

Weather Forecast

Summer heatwaves are often brought to an end by violent thunderstorms associated with a non-frontal low moving up from northern France. The afternoon will become increasingly uncomfortable as temperature and humidity levels reach their peak. In this unstable atmosphere thundery outbreaks are likely almost anywhere south of a line from the Wash westward to the Bristol Channel.

Storms are most likely to develop in the early evening following the peak in temperature and relative humidity curves when the lower atmosphere is at its most unstable. Storm cells will drift slowly north with activity lasting into the early hours of the following morning and locally through much of the following day. Once the storms have cleared there is likely to be a fresher feel to the atmosphere compared with the preceding heatwave and a westerly flow is likely to develop.

13. Slow moving cold front

Weather: Thunderstorms
Season: Summer

Synopsis

An area of high pressure that had previously dominated the British Isles is sliding away to the south-west allowing a slow moving cold front to cross the northern part of these islands. The cold front forms a distinct dividing line between the high surface temperatures developed under the anticyclone and the very much cooler and unstable Pm and Am air arriving behind the cold front from northerly latitudes.

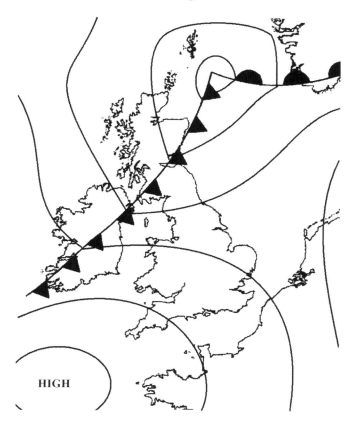

HIGH

Weather Forecast

The collision of warm and cold air masses along the steeply inclined cold front will drive rapid uplift producing thick masses of cumuliform clouds likely to generate violent thunderstorms at many points along the front. These will continue for 12-24 hours as the front slowly crosses the British Isles with widespread thunder and lightning and squally showers often producing significant accumulations over a short timescale leading to localised flooding. Hail is likely to be a feature of this activity and may cause isolated damage.

14. Frontal system crossing the British Isles (winter)

Weather: Snowy day
Season: Winter

Synopsis

An area of high pressure covering the eastern half of the British Isles begins to slide away to the east allowing the passage of an Atlantic frontal system.

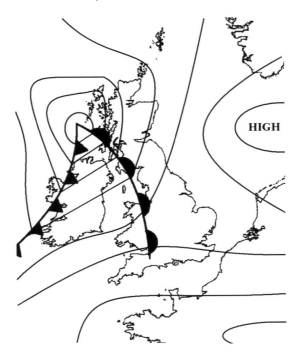

Weather Forecast

Surface temperatures have fallen considerably under the clear skies of the high pressure. As that retreats cirrus arriving from the west will be followed by lower and thicker clouds. The cooling of the lower atmosphere as the air rises along the front will be enhanced by conduction from the cold land so that when precipitation begins to fall it reaches the ground as snow. This is likely to continue for some hours until the passage of the warm front leading to considerable accumulations in some locations. Once the cold air ahead of the warm front is replaced by the milder south-westerly flow behind the front the precipitation will quickly turn to rain and in the higher temperatures, the lying snow will begin to melt.

In low temperatures a succession of frontal systems passing across the British Isles can, especially if the warm sectors are restricted in geographical extent, lead to considerable falls of snow which will continue to accumulate until there is a significant change in the synoptic situation. The nature of the snowfall varies from sustained falls along the fronts to short-lived showers in the unstable air behind a cold front. Occasionally the latter can be prolonged if individual showers coalesce.

15. Low pressure centred over the English Channel

Weather: Snowy day
Season: Winter

Synopsis

Changes in the upper atmosphere have initiated the development of an anticyclone to the north of the British Isles and temporarily pushed depression tracks further south. An occluding frontal system having passed through the Western Approaches is now driving along the English Channel. The cyclonic circulation to the north of the low centre in conjunction with the anticyclonic flow is pulling a bitterly cold easterly airstream from the continent across the southern part of the North Sea, England and on towards Wales and Ireland.

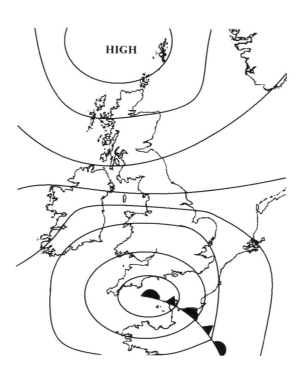

Weather Forecast

The easterly Pc air although initially very cold and relatively dry gains moisture and warmth from its passage across the North Sea and becomes unstable in its lowest layers. That drives the growth of large cumuliform clouds as the air approaches the east coast of England giving rise to significant snow showers continuing day and night. These tend to be more significant further south as the low-level inversion moves higher above the surface with increasing distance from the high pressure.

As the air moves beyond the coastal margins, the cold land removes the convective trigger so that the clouds gradually dissipate confining the heaviest falls to the eastern half of England. Renewed warming over the Irish Sea is likely to lead to snow showers along the east coast of Ireland.

16. Low pressure tracking along the western edge of the British Isles

Weather: Windy
Season: Winter half of the year

Synopsis

An intense Atlantic low pressure system (964 mb) with associated fronts has made landfall in Galway (Ireland). Propelled by a vigorous jet stream this will move north-east along the western edge of Ireland before crossing north-west Scotland and passing over the Northern Isles some twenty-four hours after reaching Ireland.

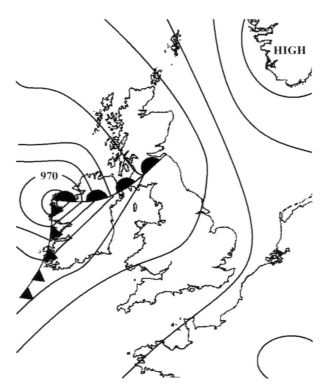

Weather Forecast

The steep pressure gradients associated with this system have developed strong surface winds over northern and western parts of the British Isles. Within 100-150 miles of the track of the low centre, winds will exceed gale force for a period of several hours. The wind direction will mainly be cyclonic meaning that the initially southerly direction backs progressively through east to north and then north-west. There will be violent squalls along the cold front and in the unstable northerly flow in the rear of the depression with the wind occasionally reaching gale force.

England and Wales will be affected by a south-westerly Tm airflow bringing low-level cloud, persistent drizzle and poor visibility although it will be relatively mild. Western Ireland and central and northern Scotland in the direct path of the fronts will experience prolonged rainfall that is often heavy. It will feel cool in the strong winds and under thick layers of cloud.

17. Low pressure passing along the northern edge of the English Channel

Weather: Windy and wet
Season: Winter half of the year

Synopsis

An Atlantic low pressure system (979 mb) has made landfall in the British Isles close to the Scilly Isles. The system, which at that point was just beginning to occlude, will move west to east along the northern edge of the English Channel before crossing into the southern part of the North Sea. The associated fronts extend southwards across the Channel into northern France.

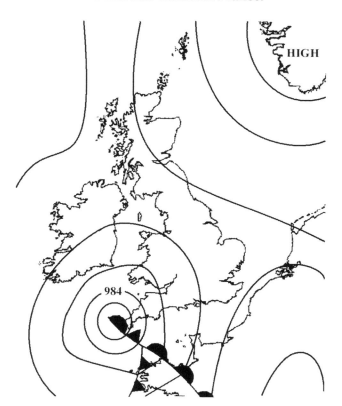

Weather Forecast

Particularly strong winds will be experienced south of a line from the middle of Cardigan Bay to the Thames Estuary. Within that area, the maximum hourly mean wind speed is likely to reach 20 kt in many locations with figures between 30-40 kt expected in exposed coastal locations such as St Catherine's Point (Isle of Wight) and Portland Bill (Dorset).

The area of significant rainfall will be broader with the highest accumulations experienced south of a line joining the Mersey and the Wash. Weather stations on high ground within that area may well record up to 50 mm in twenty-four hours with totals decreasing from south-west to north-east. Localised flooding is likely to be a serious problem.

18. High pressure centred to the west of Ireland (summer)

Weather: Sea breeze
Season: Summer

Synopsis

An anticyclone (1038 mb) is centred just beyond the south-west coast of Ireland. The high pressure extends eastward from the Atlantic, across the British Isles and northern Europe as far as the longitude of Moscow. The pressure gradient is slack in all directions with frontal systems forced to pass to the north of the British Isles.

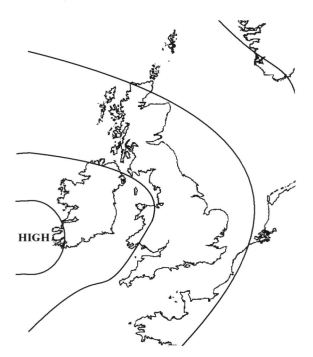

Weather Forecast

Across much of the British Isles, the day will start with clear skies and a light northerly breeze as the regional airflow circulates clockwise around the high pressure. Along the south coast of England, haze will initially cause poor visibility as the regional airflow gradually falls away to a virtual calm.

During the morning, air and land temperatures on the south coast will rise rapidly until they are 5-6 °C above those of the inshore sea surface. In these conditions, a sea breeze will develop soon after midday and gradually veer to a southerly direction under the influence of the Coriolis Force. The forward edge of the breeze will be marked by a line of cumulus indicating the sea breeze front, which by late afternoon may have moved 50 km inland. By about 1800 the difference between air and sea surface temperatures will have fallen away sufficiently to end this local circulation. During the night, a land breeze may develop in the opposite direction to that of the sea breeze.

19. Ridge of high pressure over central and southern England

Weather: Sea breeze
Season: Summer

Synopsis

A ridge of high pressure (1020 mb) extends south-west to north-east across central and southern parts of the British Isles with areas to the north occupied by a col. Frontal systems are displaced some distance to the north of their usual track and consequently have little effect on most of the region.

Weather Forecast

The weak pressure gradients across virtually the whole of the British Isles are producing very light winds highly variable in direction. In many locations but especially along the south coast, the wind will fall away to calm. Although this suggests the development of a sea breeze, it is possible that on a particular day the temperature difference between the land, the overlying air, and the sea surface in the early morning is only about 2 °C. Initially that will allow no more than a hesitant and weak sea breeze to develop. However, if the land-sea temperature contrast increases sufficiently under clear skies a southerly sea breeze will develop along the south coast with winds reaching a maximum of 10 kt. The breeze will disappear by about 1800 and later may be replaced by a land breeze moving towards the coast.

20. Family of depressions tracking across the British Isles

Weather: Cloud and rain
Season: Winter

Synopsis

A family of depressions is tracking in a north-easterly direction across northern and western parts of the British Isles. The primary depression with its centre close to the Orkney Islands is beginning to occlude. A secondary depression with its centre over Northern Ireland has formed on the trailing edge of the cold front of the primary. The secondary in its turn has a trailing cold front that has given rise to a centre of low pressure located to the west of Ireland. There is an area of higher pressure over south-east England.

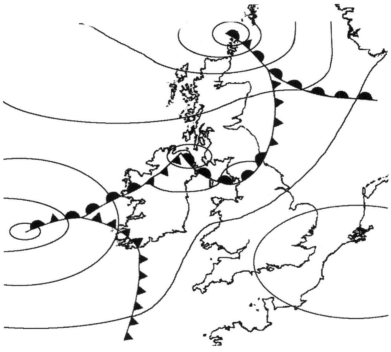

Weather Forecast

Areas to the north and west of the Tees-Exe line will experience overcast skies with varying amounts of rain, which will intensify with the passage of each front. Most of Scotland will be cool and blustery in a north-westerly airstream with significant shower activity especially along northern and western coasts. Inland areas and the east coast will be drier with more broken cloud and only scattered showers.

Much of Ireland will experience dark skies and heavy persistent rainfall with the passage of the fronts. The greater part of Wales and the English Midlands will experience low cloud with occasional drizzle in a mild south-westerly airstream. South-east England under the influence of high pressure extending from the continent will be dry with light winds and broken cloud.

Chapter Thirteen

Visual Signs

A number of visual signs including changing cloud type, wind direction and strength at various heights and pressure changes help us to predict local weather.

First Signs of a Depression

The arrival of a depression is heralded by various changes including an increase in cloud depth, thickness and cover, falling pressure and the wind backing and freshening.

Contrails

The first evidence of an approaching depression is often the presence of aircraft contrails close to the tropopause indicating that the air is relatively moist at high altitude. A fast moving jet stream creates 'turret tops' along the back of the contrails and if these trails are persistent, cirrus are probably not far away. When the trail cuts across the wind it shreds and widens sideways showing both the direction and approximate speed of the wind at that altitude, which is usually 6-10 km above the surface. Holding your thumb at arm's length and measuring the time for a patch of contrail or cirrus to pass the nail gives an idea of their speed and therefore that of the wind. Eight seconds equates to about 70 kt and five seconds suggests 100 kt. An equally rough guide to the speed is that if you detect rapid movement in the cirrus the speed is in excess of 100 kt. When their movement is only just visible, the speed is in excess of 75 kt but less than 100 kt.

Cirriform clouds

Cirrus and cirrostratus developing above the north-west horizon is a good indicator of a warm front some 900-1000 km or about 18-24 hours distance. Cirrus consists of a head from which a shower of fine ice crystals falls in a gentle arc curving away from the high altitude wind. When cirrus tails have a very shallow angle, giving a more obviously hooked appearance it indicates strong wind at that level and the probability that a high speed jet and vigorous depression are involved. This is also true if the cirrus merge into long banners stretching from horizon to horizon.

At this stage small cumulus persist in the cooler polar air at the surface. Increasingly shallow as the front approaches these can initially produce showers but as cirriform clouds spread to cover about half the sky, they are thick enough to prevent convection causing the cumulus to fragment and disappear.

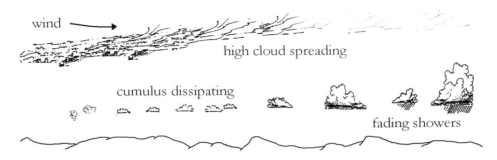

Cirrus associated with a depression usually come from the north-west or west but if they come from the north-east they are unlikely to foretell the arrival of a depression. When the cirrus trails hang straight down and there is clearly no wind shear (change of velocity with height) the weather is unlikely to deteriorate.

Cross-Winds' Rule

Meteorologists refer to the 'cross-winds' rule where clouds following cirrus associated with a depression come progressively from the west and then the south-west because the wind in the lower atmosphere is strongly backed from the jet.

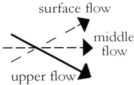

In a vigorous system there is a progressive blending of one cloud type with the next so that cirrus eventually merge into long banners stretching from horizon to horizon creating a layer of cirrostratus covering the whole sky with a halo around the sun or moon. The altostratus sky following the cirriform has a watery appearance with the sun and moon only visible as if seen through ground glass. The longer the build-up of this succession of clouds the more likely the system will be extensive and intense.

Gales

The initial fall in pressure is erratic but usually about 0.40 mb/hour increasing to 0.50 mb/hour and perhaps 1.25-1.40 mb/hour if a storm is approaching. The greater the fall in pressure the more likely the wind will be strong. A fall of 3 mb in three hours suggests a strengthening of the wind while a fall of more than 5 mb in three hours produces a force six. When pressure falls over 9 mb in three hours a gale is more or less certain and if the local wind is force three or less when these falls are observed you have about four to eight hours warning. A total fall of 10-20 mb is possible.

Only 20-25% of depressions bring gale force winds. Gales rarely last more than twenty-four hours because of the rapid movement of frontal systems although if a series of intense depressions pass in quick succession prolonged gales are likely. Gales are more likely in winter because the larger temperature gradients at that time cause more pronounced convergence along the polar front. They are more common in north-west parts of the British Isles because the mean depression track tends to be to the north of a line through the English Midlands. Even in winter gales are infrequent in southern England.

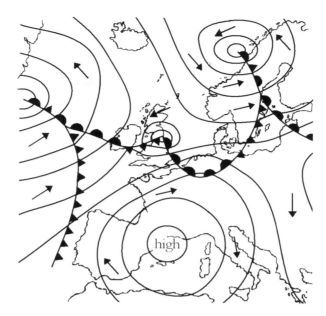

The fact that the barometer is steady does not rule out the possibility of increasing wind strength in the near future. Some of the heaviest gales occur after pressure has stopped falling and gales accompanied by rapidly rising pressure are generally more squally.

Warm Front

As the front approaches the wind veers so that a southerly or south-westerly wind before the warm front veers to the south-west or west during the one or maybe two hours it takes the frontal zone to pass. The strength that increases as the front approaches usually decreases behind the front.

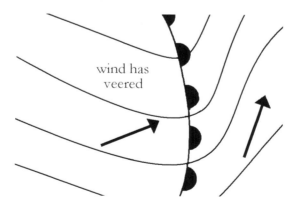

The passage of the warm front follows a period of possibly four to five hours of continuous rain from dark nimbostratus. When the front passes the rain stops, the cloud base rises and there can be patches of clear sky. The wind may well continue to veer as the front passes but the pressure usually falls more slowly.

Cold Front

The low stratus of the warm sector can hide the approach of the cold front with its great banks of cumulus and nimbostratus. However, one indicator of its approach is cirrus streaming ahead of rounded cumulus tops. The front comes from the left (your right-hand) of the surface wind as you look into it so if the present wind is south-westerly the front will arrive from the west or north-west at a speed of 25-30 kt.

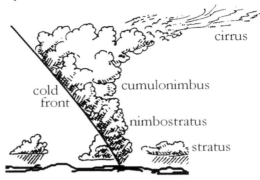

Where the depression is part of a family the next low follows soon after the cold front has passed with the cirrus to the rear of the clearing cold front moving in the same direction as the surface wind. In that situation the high cloud dampens the showers you normally expect behind a cold front.

Occlusion

The approach of an occlusion is heralded by a rapid change from cirrus to cirrostratus then altostratus with gaps in the cloud cover more likely than with a depression. With an old occlusion all three clouds and stratocumulus can occupy the sky at the same time.

Clouds

Clouds can be used to forecast changes in the weather both in the short term and over a period of several hours. More specifically stratus indicates a stable moist atmosphere and if they are very low they suggest the possible development of fog and calms. When the stratus is broken into bands which are moving the arrival of a band can be accompanied by a slight veer in the direction of the wind.

Convective Showers / Thunderstorms

Cumuliform clouds are indicative of unstable air. Over land, they tend to grow rapidly in the afternoon whereas over the sea they are just as likely to develop in the morning or at night. In coastal regions such clouds can develop over the sea and neighbouring land at the same time.

Small cumulus only 2-300 m deep in the early afternoon are indicative of fine weather but if they attain that depth during the morning and continue to grow they are likely to develop into larger cumulus or cumulonimbus and the weather is likely to turn squally possibly with heavy showers.

In situations other than thermal uplift, cumulonimbus can develop either in association with a cold front or a trough. Following the predicted arrival of one of these, a line of towering cumulus on the north-west horizon in the absence of cirrus or a significant fall in pressure indicates the approach of a squall lasting perhaps twenty to thirty minutes. The imminent arrival of a squall is suggested by fuzzy grey stalks in the distance, indicating rain falling from distant clouds.

Quiet Weather

The development of quiet weather is less easy to predict. Where pressure is steady at 1020 mb or rising beyond that the quiet weather is likely to last for at least twenty-four hours. The folklore 'red sky at night shepherd's delight' is well founded because the red sky is produced by the light of the setting sun reflecting off clouds breaking up over the western horizon as a trough or cold front clears to the east. The reverse equally holds true so that at dawn clouds building on the western horizon indicating the approach of a depression are brilliantly lit by the rising sun giving credence to 'red sky in the morning, shepherd's warning'.

strongly hooked cirrus indicating strong winds at altitude
associated with approaching frontal system

weather balloon

Chapter Fourteen

Commercial Forecasting

In all parts of the world weather forecasting begins with observations made at regular intervals either by unmanned automatic weather stations (AWS) or by humans working in a variety of situations. These are supplemented by data from aircraft, ships, satellites, rainfall radar and radiosonde attached to meteorological balloons. All this information is transmitted at regular intervals to weather centres such as the Exeter headquarters of the UK Meteorological Office where it is processed.

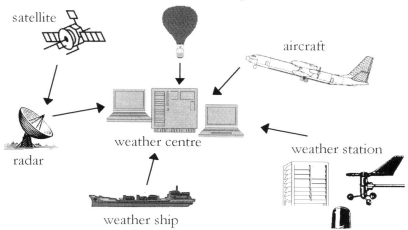

UK Meteorological Office

Every day the Exeter supercomputers receive more than half a million observations from locations scattered across the globe. Within the borders of the UK the Met Office has a network of more than 200 AWS deliberately positioned about 40 km apart so that while not duplicating observations they produce a network of sufficient density to keep a close watch on all parts of the weather systems that are the key to the day-to-day weather of the British Isles. The AWS record a wide range of different elements with the most important for short-term forecasting being temperature, pressure, rainfall, wind speed and direction, humidity, cloud height and visibility. This data is recorded at one minute intervals, auto logged and transmitted immediately to Exeter.

Siting of Weather Stations

Sympathetic siting of a weather station is very important and in recent years, poorly sited stations have been mapped by climate change sceptics to suggest that global warming is in effect a recording error. Whatever the merits of the climate change debate, weather forecasts will be less accurate if based on data from poorly sited stations.

The chosen site must as far as possible be representative of the geography of the area that it represents. Obviously if it were shown to be in an isolated hotspot or unduly affected by cold air drainage compared with the average of the area it represents then any forecast may or may not be accurate for the weather station but would almost certainly be inaccurate for the wider area. Equally, a site on or close to the top of a ridge will be misleading because average wind strength tends to be stronger in such locations. The reverse would equally apply in a sheltered leeward hollow, which might be misleadingly affected by a local föhn effect. While it is important for weather stations to be in and around urban areas the precise site must not be such that the instruments are unduly affected by warmth emitted by heating ducts or indirectly from walls or sunlight reflected from the mass of glass that dominates modern buildings. It is also important to locate an urban weather station in such a way that it is not affected by accelerated airflow (canyoning) between high buildings.

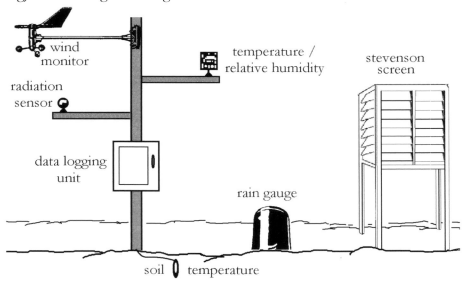

Supercomputers

All data arriving at Exeter goes through a rigorous quality control procedure before being sent to the relevant Met Office supercomputer, which can smoothly work through some one hundred trillion calculations in a second. Such speed allows the input of perhaps half a million observations from across the globe. It is this data input that is the starting point for running forecast models each containing more than one million lines of code.

Numerical Weather Prediction

Weather forecasting today is dominated by mathematical models of the atmosphere developed over several decades through the construction of equations representing various laws of physics. In effect, a completed model consists of a set of equations awaiting the input of the observational data that allows the model to resolve the equations into a forecast (prediction) for a given area and time frame.

Grid

The very nature of the Earth-Atmosphere system demands that it be divided into discrete blocks with horizontal and vertical elements to ease the handling of data input and the resulting forecast. This is achieved by dividing the atmosphere into a number of horizontal layers and the surface into a grid of boxes with the number of each varying according to the nature and complexity of the model.

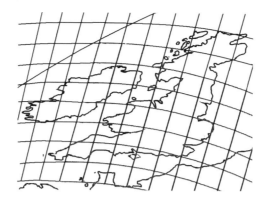

The number of boxes and layers is limited in part by the time required to run a programme. Obviously, the equations have to be resolved sufficiently far in advance for a forecast to be made, analysed and then distributed before the weather arrives and that limits the density of the boxes and layers. The most widely used global model has a resolution of about 40 km over the British Isles and even that requires in excess of 150 million equations to be resolved to move the atmosphere forward by just fifteen minutes.

While there is always an element of uncertainty in even a short-range forecast the level of uncertainty for a particular weather event is usually fairly predictable over a period of two or three days. A forecaster might for example, predict that a given part of a depression will pass over Dublin in 66-72 hours with an estimated 70% degree of certainty. However, beyond seventy-two hours the degree of certainty falls away rapidly.

Local Forecasts

The forecast produced by a numerical model is a picture of the weather averaged over a grid box so it is vitally important that the recipient of the forecast understands that the observed weather at any one point within the box may not necessarily be as predicted. This is the reason why media forecasts do not appear to be necessarily correct on every occasion because if for example showers are forecast in (say) south-east Ireland it obviously does not mean that every single location within that area will directly experience or perhaps even see a shower.

The typical shower covers little more than 1 km^2 (0.4 $miles^2$) which is a tiny fraction of the area of the British Isles about (317 000 km^2 /122 000 $miles^2$). Even if that shower drifts 60 km (23 miles) on the wind it will affect only a tiny fraction of 1% of the total land area. Trying to forecast the precise area affected by such a shower is impossible.

The professional forecaster employed by the Met Office or any other organisation has to use his/her skills in a highly subjective manner to interpret the grid box forecast for a more precise location. This is achieved through background knowledge of the geography of an area and the level of accuracy of previously modelled forecasts for the same area in similar atmospheric circumstances.

Long-Range Forecasts

The Met Office in recent years has been criticised for the accuracy of its long-range forecasts particularly the infamous 'barbecue summer' of 2010. The public relations department of the Met Office made a colossal mistake using such a phrase perhaps not realising how it would be reported by the popular media. There is also considerable misunderstanding by the media and the wider population of the true nature of long-term forecasts, which should be seen as computer-generated predictions of what the most complex mathematical models suggest is likely to happen. There is no way of predicting the weather for more than a few days ahead with any degree of certainty but the media ignores that.

The problem faced by forecasters across the world is that the global atmosphere and oceans exist in a non-linear chaotic system so that it is unlikely that scientists will ever be in a position to predict a single weather event months ahead. The best that can be achieved at present is to run models in such a way as to predict a statistical description of the weather several months in advance. This in effect is what occurred with the 'barbecue summer' when the Met Office forecasters predicted that a summer with average or above average temperatures was highly probable, which proved to be a fair description of the summer of 2010. Unfortunately, they did not predict the lengthy periods of cloudy weather and occasional rainy outbreaks that did not fit in with the media idea of a 'barbecue summer'.

computers are used for climate modelling and day-to-day forecasting

UK Meteorological Office Website

(www.metoffice.gov.uk)

The website of the Met Office offers a comprehensive weather forecast service for UK residents and visitors plus a vast amount of information about weather and climatology in general including detailed information on a range of issues such as climate change. The home page includes links to Ultra Violet Forecasts, Space Weather Forecasts (for example solar flare activity) and Event Forecasts such as for the Ashes (cricket!).

The range of forecasts includes predictions for one to two days in advance, three to five days, six to fifteen days and sixteen to thirty days. The two shorter periods can be related to specific regions of the UK and even cities and towns whereas the two longer periods predict the weather for the UK as a whole. The level of accuracy of the forecasts inevitably falls away with increasing time scale but the one to two day forecast can generally be relied upon assuming that they are carefully interpreted by the user.

The website also offers the latest Atlantic surface pressure charts, which can be advanced in twelve hour steps up to eighty-four hours ahead. The rainfall radar and satellite images are very useful when deciding whether the immediate weather is 'fit to go'. The latest observations let you know how various parts of the UK are faring.

Met Éireann Website

(www.met.ie)

The National Meteorological Service of Ireland is part of the Department of the Environment, Heritage and Local Government. Visitors to its website will find on the home page brief forecasts for the day in question, with links to forecasts for the following day and the outlook for the next five to seven days. An annotated map shows how weather, temperature and wind are likely to change over the next five days. A thumbnail of the latest rainfall radar links to a larger map, which shows the rainfall over the preceding six hours. A thumbnail of the latest satellite image links to a larger copy of the same image.

There are left-hand-side links to a number of useful pages including Atlantic charts that show the movement of frontal systems, bands of rainfall and changes of temperature over a period of forty-eight hours. There are also useful weather station reports so you can see where the sun is shining and buoy reports give an idea of sea conditions allowing the observer to assess how the weather is likely to change in the coming hours. The whole country rainfall radar, which can be animated over a period of several hours, also helps to show the changing weather patterns as do the satellite images.

At the foot of the left-hand side, a link takes the visitor to the Monthly Weather Bulletin, which provides a summary of the weather of the past month and that of other months, seasons and years through a drop-down menu.

Chapter Fifteen

Media Forecasts

The public can obtain daily and longer-term forecasts from a variety of media sources including television, radio, newspapers and of course the World Wide Web. While many of these derive their forecasts directly from the Met Office there is a growing number of private companies that provide a professional forecast, which are most likely to be found through a dedicated website.

BBC Weather Centre

The BBC Weather Centre provides forecasts for the television channels BBC1, BBC2 and BBC24 and the radio stations Radio1, Radio2, Radio4, Radio5 Live and 6Music. The forecasters seen and heard on the BBC are all professionals trained by the UK Met Office and subsequently seconded to work for the BBC where they present radio and television forecasts from a studio in the BBC Weather Centre. Data from the supercomputer in Exeter is transmitted directly to the computers in the BBC Weather Centre.

Television Forecasts

The data received from Exeter is processed by the 'Weatherscape XT' graphics system, which allows the forecaster to put together the graphics display seen by the viewer. The graphics system allows the forecaster to put together a sequence of charts and other graphics to present a clear forecast. The display includes a mix of text characteristics, still and animated images including those submitted by viewers, video clips and live webcam pictures. The land area of the islands is displayed as a rather dry brown colour giving a good contrast with the graphics.

The graphics display prepared for the next broadcast to be seen by the public is projected onto a translucent screen as an exceedingly faint image that is just distinct enough for the forecaster to know where he/she is pointing. This is flooded with blue or green light because camera technology allows that to be transmitted as a perfect image of the graphics. It is important that the forecaster does not dress in either of those colours otherwise he/she will disappear into the display. The forecaster reads the autocue while holding a remote control with which the display is paused or moved on as required.

Radio Forecasts

In most respects, the preparation of a radio forecast is the same as for television with the exception that the forecaster has to paint a picture in words for the listener and that is a much more difficult task. Radio forecasts include the iconic Shipping Forecast first produced in 1864 and broadcast on the BBC since 1924. This is such a significant part of the culture of these islands that concerns were expressed on May 30th 2014 when the BBC failed to broadcast the 0520 Shipping Forecast. Fortunately this was due to a technical error rather than some unimaginative change to the radio schedules.

BBC Mobile

The BBC website provides a forecast service for mobile phones. A simple uncluttered page links the visitor to a page detailing the up-to-date British Isles forecast as well as the Shipping Forecast and any UK weather warnings. A search facility allows the visitor to find the forecast for a particular location in the UK. Depending on the mobile contract there may be a charge for this service.

Further details on the BBC mobile weather services can be found at

www.bbc.co.uk/weather

and scroll down to the 'Mobile site' link at the foot of the page or,

Go to the web application on your mobile phone menu and type in

m.bbc.co.uk/weather

BBC Website Weather Pages

(http://www.bbc.co.uk/weather)

The home page of the weather section of the BBC website displays a short description of the predicted weather for the day accompanied by a simple map. Clicking on 'More UK Weather' opens a page with a map of the British Isles identical to that used in television broadcasts with bands of cloud and rainfall shown and the temperature for the UK capitals and Manchester. On the right-hand-side of the page there is a video link giving the same forecast but in more detail. Clicking on the 'Pressure' tab at the top of the page opens a simplified synoptic map of the Atlantic and western Europe including the British Isles.

The 'Coast and Sea' link on the home page leads to the Coastal Area, Inshore Weather and Shipping Forecasts as well as tide tables.

Radio 4 Broadcasts

The most comprehensive of the radio forecasts are those on Radio 4, which can be found at

FM 92.4-94.6
on DAB Radio as Radio4, BBC Radio4 or Radio4
MHz LW 198kHz
MW 720kHz
Sky 0104
Freeview/Freesat 704
Virgin 904
(further details bbc.co.uk/radio4)

The complete Radio4 schedule of weather forecasts (August 2015) is detailed below:

Monday to Saturday

0030 weather forecast broadcast after midnight news
0048 Shipping Forecast (on FM and LW)
0520 Shipping Forecast (on FM and LW)
0556 the latest weather forecast for farmers
0606 weather forecast broadcast within the Today programme (not Sunday)
0657 weather forecast broadcast within the Today programme
0757 weather forecast broadcast within the Today programme
1200 Shipping Forecast follows news headlines (LW only)
1257 weather forecast
1754 Shipping Forecast LW only on weekdays (FM and LW at weekend)
1757 weather forecast

RTÉ (Radió Teillifís Éireann)

(www.rte.ie)

RTÉ, the National Public Service Broadcaster of Ireland, has a weather section responsible for the production of forecasts for its website, television and radio channels.

Website

The RTÉ website presents the weather forecast in pictorial maps illustrating the predicted weather for the day in question and that for the following day accompanied by brief text. Similar information is on separate pages for the regions of Ireland and there is a brief three-day outlook.

The left-hand-side of the page has links to the marine forecast as well as charts for today and tomorrow, which display the forecast position of surface pressure values, frontal systems, rainfall and cloud belts and probable temperature.

Radio and Television

The radio and television forecast transmission times are

RTÉ Radio One

0602 sea area forecast
0755 morning forecast and outlook for the coming days
1253 land and sea area forecast
1755 evening forecast and outlook for the coming days
2355 late night land and sea area forecast

(the evening forecast times vary at weekends due to sports coverage)

RTÉ Television

1105 weather forecast for today and tomorrow
1150 weather forecast for today and tomorrow
1315 weather forecast for this afternoon, tonight and next two days
1545 weather forecast for tonight and next three days
1750 European forecast with Irish update
1850 weather forecast for tomorrow and next two days (summer time 1825)
2125 three day weather forecast
2300 European forecast with Irish weather (RTÉ Two)
0000 three day weather forecast (times vary for late night forecast)

Forecasts do depend on running time of news broadcasts. On Saturday and Sunday times vary with RTÉ One broadcasting the Farming Forecast at lunchtime on Sunday.

UK Newspapers

Several newspapers provide detailed weather information including forecasts and reports from the previous day. The weather section in the Times is typical of several broadsheets in that it includes five small maps of the British Isles showing the predicted weather for the next five days. This includes temperature, rainfall, sun or cloud and a brief description of the likely weather. A larger map shows the weather prediction for the day of publication, which includes the same elements plus the sea state and a more detailed text. There is also an Atlantic pressure chart for that day again with brief text. The weather page on the Times also includes weather reports from some fifty locations across the British Isles for the preceding twenty-four hours. The times of sunrise and sunset are given and there is tidal information for some locations.

Under the heading 'Weather Eye' a particular aspect of weather is discussed. It may be some comment on the weather for the next few days or the weather of the recent past if it has been noteworthy. There are also occasional short pieces relating aspects of weather to historical events such as how conditions might have favoured one side or the other in a particular battle or military campaign.

Irish Newspapers

The Irish Times (www.irishtimes.com/weather) has useful weather information on its website with an essentially pictorial representation of the predicted weather forecast for the next five days at Dublin and many other locations accessed through a drop-down menu.

Private Companies

There are a number of private companies in both the UK and Ireland and indeed across the globe that now provide extensive weather services. These include

Meteo Group/Weathercast   www.weathercast.co.uk
XCV Weather   www.xcvweather.co.uk
Weather Online   www.weatheronline.co.uk

Useful Websites

➢ **www.bbc.co.uk/weather**

This is a good companion to the radio and TV forecasts on BBC.

➢ **www.met.ie**

This is a good companion to the radio and TV forecasts on RTÉ

➢ **www.metoffice.gov.uk**

The UK Meteorological Office website has a number of excellent pages including rainfall radar and satellite images.

➢ **www.xcweather.co.uk**

Latest observations and forecasts in the British Isles.

➢ **www.weathercast.co.uk**

Latest observations and forecasts in the British Isles.

➢ **www.weatheronline.co.uk/weather/maps**

Latest observations and forecasts in the British Isles.

➢ **www.weather.com**

Latest observations and forecasts in the British Isles. (select the link in the top right hand corner)

➢ **www.opc.ncep.noaa.gov/A_sfc_full_ocean.jpg**

This is an excellent webpage displaying the most recent North Atlantic surface pressure chart.

➢ **www.netweather.tv/index.cgi?action=jetstream**

This page on a commercial website displays the latest position of the jet stream.

➢ **www.met.rdg.ac.uk/~brugge/col.html**

This is the website of the Climatological Observers Link (COL)

> ➢ **www.theweatherclub.org.uk**

This is the website of the Weather Club, which issues a regular magazine.

> ➢ **www.weathershop.co.uk**

One of several commercial websites retailing weather instruments.

> ➢ **www.greatweather.co.uk**

An excellent portal for a range of websites.

There are many more sites to be found !

Tabbed Pages

There is something to be said for having one browser dedicated to weather sites so that when selected it opens with a number of tabs each linking to a different weather site. Suggestions include:

http://www.metoffice.gov.uk/public/weather/observation/

This opens to a map displaying the latest weather across the British Isles. A search box allows you to go to a detailed observation and forecast page for your particular location.

http://www.metoffice.gov.uk/public/weather/observation/map

This opens a map on which you can display various weather elements including rainfall and wind. The drop-down menu also gives access to satellite images.

http://www.weatheronline.co.uk

Navigate the 'Forecast' and 'Week ahead' links to find the forecast for the coming week.

http://www.metoffice.gov.uk/public/weather/surface-pressure

This provides a map of the present sea level pressure including weather systems.

http://www.weathercharts.org/ukmomslp

This opens to a number of sea level pressure maps for the next six days.

http://squall.sfsu.edu/crws/jetstream_fcsts.html

Selecting 'Initial analysis' opens a map of the current jet stream.

Units Used

Imperial and Metric

In the UK many people and indeed organisations still use a mix of imperial and metric units and that is even more so the case when talking about the weather. It is important to pay close attention to the system used in a particular situation. Media forecasts invariably use metric for precipitation although the imperial conversion is often given – especially when a specific event produces a large total.

Imperial / Metric Units

The imperial system of weights and measures fell out of fashion in science throughout the world during the later decades of the twentieth century and much of the non-scientific world beyond the UK and North America had always used the metric system. It is mostly in the UK and North America that a degree of overlap between the two systems remains.

In the UK, metric has been taught and examined to the exclusion of the imperial system for many decades although the general population still moves – often with some confusion – between the two. It is probably in distance, height and speed that most overlap occurs and will probably do so for many years to come. Aviation law illustrates this perfectly with reference in the same sentence to horizontal distance from cloud in metres and vertical distance from cloud in feet. Contours on aviation charts continue to be shown in feet yet Ordnance Survey maps have displayed contours in metres for several decades although walkers and climbers still think of summits as being over 2000 feet (say) rather than 609 metres. There is similar confusion with regard to road traffic where the British stick resolutely to mph and think of distance in terms of miles but buy fuel by the litre and then convert to mpg (miles per gallon). It is probably only in money that the metric system is firmly established – it is just so much simpler than pounds, shillings and pence!

Conversion

There is a temptation when writing to place a conversion in brackets after the relevant dimension but that interrupts the smooth flow of a sentence – and which goes in brackets? Imperial or metric? How precise do you make the conversion without writing a figure that includes a decimal point?

There are few hard and fast rules but as a rule use the metric version and place the imperial conversion in brackets – once only. Do not convert every occurrence and avoid trying to be too precise – that creates ugly looking figures – 10 000 m (= 32 808.399 feet!). Write the first occurrence as 10 000 m (33 000 feet) and the reader will almost certainly realise that the conversion has been rounded up (or down).

A common conversion that is gradually disappearing and should not be used is to place the Fahrenheit equivalent in brackets after a temperature in Celsius. An exception would be when writing for an American audience who are still accustomed to Fahrenheit in media forecasts. Even in the imperial stronghold of the UK Celsius is widely understood and used.

Units and Prefixes

The metric system consists of units and prefixes. The unit represents a measure of a physical property such as area, length, power, time or volume while the prefix represents a method of multiplying or dividing the unit by 10, 100 or 1000 and so on. The prefix and unit combine to form a single word as in

kilometre	kilo	= 1000 (prefix)	metre (unit)
kilogram	kilo	= 1000 (prefix)	gram (unit)
megawatt	mega	= 1 000 000 (prefix)	watt (unit)

Symbols

The metric system as was the case with the imperial system makes considerable use of symbols to ease the burden on both writer and reader. They are usually lower case except where the unit is named after an individual so it is 'm for metre' but 'C' for Coulomb (a measure of electric charge). The symbol for 1 000 000 (M – Mega) or more is always displayed in capitals while that for 1000 (k – kilo) or less is lower case.

Symbols are never pluralised 21 km (not 21 kms) and a full stop should not be used with a symbol other than at the end of a sentence. Commas can create ambiguity so use a non-breaking space as the thousands separator (10 000 not 10,000) although it is accepted practice to have no separator if there are only four digits in the number (9000 not 9 000). Note that a forward slash must always be used for per ie km/h not km per h, which looks ugly. If type setting allows, a space should always be created between the number and the unit so that you would expect to see 25 cm (not 25cm) and 37 °C (not 37°C).

As far as possible avoid using large numbers. Therefore, in preference use 1 m rather than 100 cm and 5 km rather than 5000 m although in athletics a commentator would be likely to refer to a 5000 m or even 5 k race (you would not – hopefully – see the latter written). Note that it is sometimes better to use a long number if a decimal is involved so you might measure a length of wood as 350 cm rather than 3.5 m.

Finally note that symbols and abbreviations are not the same although particularly when taking notes it can seem that way. The correct usage of the symbol 'm' is to represent metres not miles or millions.

Superscript Numbers

Superscript numbers appear quite often in meteorology so it is helpful to understand their meaning. In mathematical terms the superscript number is known as a power (exponent or index). If it is positive then it tells you how many times the base number is multiplied by itself:

the positive exponent formula is $a^n = a \times a \times a \ldots n$ times

For example 2^4 is equal to 2 x 2 x 2 x 2 = 16.

$10^2 = 10 \times 10 = 100$
$10^4 = 10 \times 10 \times 10 \times 10 = 10\ 000$

However, if the superscript number is preceded by a minus sign that tells you how many times the base number is divided by itself:

the negative exponent formula is $a^{-n} = 1 / a^n$ so,

$10^{-2} = 1 / 10^2 = 1 / 100 = .01$
$10^{-4} = 1 / 10^4 = 1 / 10\,000 = .0001$

Speed

This can be shown quite simply so that,

1 ms = 3.6 kph = 1.94 kt (or kn) = 2.24 mph

Meteorologists use metres per second (ms) for wind strength while media forecasts and the public tend to use mph presumably because that allows a quick comparison with vehicle speed. However, seafarers use knots and the Beaufort Scale.

Diameter

When discussing small elements such as condensation nuclei and cloud drops the standard imperial and metric units in use throughout the world are of little use because these features are microscopically small. It is the micron (μm) that is used by meteorologists to describe these elements with the relationship between that and more easily recognisable metric units given below -

1 μm (micron) = 0.001 mm = 10^{-6} m
1000 μm = 1.0 mm = 0.1 cm
10 000 μm = 1.0 cm

Atmospheric Pressure

Most readers will be familiar with the household barometer, which displays pressure in inches although that is no longer used in forecasts or meteorology in general. Media forecasts use the millibar with mean sea level pressure being equal to 1013.25 millibars. Meteorologists use the term hectopascal (hPa) which fortunately is the direct equivalent of the millibar, so

1000 hPa = 1000 mb
1013 hPa = 1013 mb

Weight

In meteorology, weight is most frequently used when discussing the amount of water vapour in the atmosphere. Metric units are widely used so that we refer to the number of grams (g) of water vapour in a kilogram (kg) of dry air.

Celsius to Fahrenheit											
°C	°F	°C	°F	°C	°F	°C	°F	°C	°F	°C	°F
-20	-04	-10	14	00	32	10	50	20	68	30	86
-19	-02	-09	16	01	34	11	52	21	70	31	88
-18	00	-08	18	02	36	12	54	22	72	32	90
-17	01	-07	19	03	37	13	55	23	73	33	91
-16	03	-06	21	04	39	14	57	24	75	34	93
-15	05	-05	23	05	41	15	59	25	77	35	95
-14	07	-04	25	06	43	16	61	26	79	36	97
-13	09	-03	27	07	45	17	63	27	81	37	99
-12	10	-02	28	08	46	18	64	28	82	38	100
-11	12	-01	30	09	48	19	66	29	84	39	102

Millimetres to Inches									
mm	ins	mm	ins	mm	ins	mm	ins	mm	ins
1	0.0394	21	0.8268	41	1.6142	61	2.4016	81	3.1890
2	0.0787	22	0.8661	42	1.6535	62	2.4409	82	3.2283
3	0.1181	23	0.9055	43	1.6929	63	2.4803	83	3.2677
4	0.1575	24	0.9449	44	1.7323	64	2.5197	84	3.3071
5	0.1969	25	0.9843	45	1.7717	65	2.5591	85	3.3465
6	0.2362	26	1.0236	46	1.8110	66	2.5984	86	3.3858
7	0.2756	27	1.0630	47	1.8504	67	2.6378	87	3.4252
8	0.3150	28	1.1024	48	1.8898	68	2.6772	88	3.4646
9	0.3543	29	1.1417	49	1.9291	69	2.7165	89	3.5039
10	0.3937	30	1.1811	50	1.9685	70	2.7559	90	3.5433
11	0.4331	31	1.2205	51	2.0079	71	2.7953	91	3.5827
12	0.4724	32	1.2598	52	2.0472	72	2.8346	92	3.6220
13	0.5118	33	1.2992	53	2.0866	73	2.8740	93	3.6614
14	0.5512	34	1.3386	54	2.1260	74	2.9134	94	3.7008
15	0.5906	35	1.3780	55	2.1654	75	2.9528	95	3.7402
16	0.6299	36	1.4173	56	2.2047	76	2.9921	96	3.7795
17	0.6693	37	1.4567	57	2.2441	77	3.0315	97	3.8189
18	0.7087	38	1.4961	58	2.2835	78	3.0709	98	3.8583
19	0.7480	39	1.5354	59	2.3228	79	3.1102	99	3.8976
20	0.7874	40	1.5748	60	2.3622	80	3.1496	100	3.9370

Beaufort Scale

Beaufort Scale

Beaufort is a visual descriptive scale that relates movement in the natural and human landscape to the passage of air allowing the display of a numerical relationship between wind strength and visual criteria. Although the Beaufort Scale dates from 1806 it can be assumed that similar scales have existed for hundreds if not thousands of years. The great seafarers of the past, Phoenician, Viking, Venetian, Portuguese and many others, would have made use of short descriptive phrases recalling repeated scenes at sea in terms of wave size, forces on the boat and the amount of canvas that could be carried. Almost certainly those working the land would have had similar scales related to the movement of leaves, branches and trees and smoke. Sadly, such scales were not written down or at least they have not survived.

Daniel Defoe (c1661-1731)

Daniel Defoe wrote an astonishingly detailed account of the devastating storm that crossed the southern half of the British Isles on 26-27th November 1703. This and his naturalist writing encouraged him to devise a twelve point scale relating wind strength to phrases used by seafarers at that time. It is possible he was also influenced by the late seventeenth century logs of the privateer William Dampier.

Stark calm	A topsail gale
Calm weather	Blows fresh
Little wind	A hard gale of wind
A fine breeze	A fret of wind
A small gale	A storm
A fresh gale	A tempest

The eighteenth century was very much the heyday of the amateur naturalist especially among the clergy and country squires who wrote incredibly detailed accounts of the natural landscape, which would include references to the weather. They would have been aware of the writing of Defoe and probably of his scale to which they would have added references to movement in the natural landscape, as a way to record changing wind strength.

In the mid-eighteenth century the civil engineer John Smeaton while designing and building windmills invented an anemometer in an attempt to understand more fully the relationship between wind strength and the rotation of the sails of a windmill. In line with this he developed a wind scale based on the relationship between wind strength, movement in the landscape and the speed of rotation of a windmill.

Towards the end of the century, quantitative versions of the scale began to appear in commercial vessels and warships. The East India Company was to the fore with its Hydrographer Alex Dalrymple devising a wind scale for company captains in the early 1780s and in 1801 Colonel Capper of the same company described a quantitative scale produced by a Mr Rous. The descriptive terms used in this are very similar to those used by Beaufort who was apprenticed to the East India Company for a number of years. Capper's scale related descriptive terms to the wind strength in MPH and feet per second.

Almost calm	1 mph
Just perceptible	2-3
Gentle breeze	4-5
Fresh breeze	10-15
Fresh gale	20-25
Strong gale	30-35
Hard gale	40-45
Storm	50+
Violent hurricane, tempests, etc.	60-100

Francis Beaufort (1774-1857)

Francis Beaufort, born in Ireland, joined the East India Company at age thirteen where he would have been influenced by the work of Capper and Dalrymple. Taking command of HMS Woolwich in 1805 he was almost certainly already using the scale for which he would become famous and in January 1806 made his first reference to it in his personal seagoing log. Beaufort was not original in this idea but was part of an evolutionary process and simply reorganised collective maritime experience.

In 1807 he modified his scale to read thirteen points (0-12) and added descriptions that related wind strength to the canvas carried by a fully-rigged frigate in different weather conditions. Forces 1-4 were described in terms of such a ship under full sail on her fastest point of sailing in smooth water – what would be called a broad reach by twenty-first century yachtsmen. Force 1 would be just strong enough to 'give steerage way' while Force 2-4 saw increased boat speed. Force 5 onwards related the criteria to the need to reef specific sails. In effect this related wind strength to the amount of sail that the ship could just carry close-hauled while 'in chase, full and by'. Just as important was the implication that leaving too much canvas flying would likely lead to the loss of a spar and perhaps even a mast. In a Force 11 the ship would be reduced to storm staysails and unsurprisingly in Force 12 the ship would 'show no canvas'.

force	description	force	description
1	Calm	7	Moderate gale
2	Light air	8	Fresh gale
3	Light breeze	9	Strong gale
4	Gentle breeze	10	Whole gale
5	Moderate breeze	11	Storm
6	Fresh breeze	12	Hurricane

Beaufort's career at sea came to an end in 1812 when he was seriously injured in an engagement with Turkish forces while carrying out surveying duties. He then had a variety of roles before becoming Hydrographer of the Navy in 1829, a post he retained until his retirement in 1855. For a long time his scale remained something of a secret for no apparent reason other than a failure to promote it. There is certainly no mention of it in the logs of other ships until in his role as Hydrographer he commissioned the voyage of the Beagle (1831-36) in which the scale was used officially for what seems to have been the first time.

Beaufort and Robert FitzRoy the commander of the Beagle were good friends so the latter was probably keen to use the scale. From that point on it became widely used in the Royal Navy and in 1838 The Lords Commissioners of the Admiralty decreed that it should be used in all Royal Navy ships. Beaufort was awarded the rank of Rear Admiral in 1846 while Fitzroy became the first director of the organisation that would later become the Meteorological Office.

The Beaufort Scale was revised in 1874 to reflect changes in the rig of warships and then again in the last years of the century to take into account the rig of the fishing smack that was widely used around the coasts of the British Isles and the Thames barge (photo), which was a workhorse of coastal traffic.

The decline of commercial sailing vessels in the late nineteenth and early twentieth centuries required authorities to seek other criteria to relate to wind strength. The obvious solution was to use the state of the sea in open water but not sheltered coastal waters where tides and coastal topography affect the waves. It was the British meteorologist George Simpson who in 1906 revised the Beaufort Scale so that it was based on the sea state. Although this quickly became widely adopted by seafarers of all nations it was not adopted by the International Meteorological Association until 1939. Simpson also devised a scale for land observers.

The Beaufort Scale in its present form dates from about 1960 when it was improved with the addition of probable wave height and probable maximum wave heights.

It is perhaps surprising that the Beaufort Scale remains significant in the high technology world of the twenty-first century where wind speed can be measured to the nth degree by quite basic instruments. However the Beaufort Scale offers something that no piece of technology can offer. It describes what our senses are experiencing and that is very important to those who live and work within the natural world. It is pragmatic to use a scale that does not require mathematical precision and, because Beaufort numbers are meaningful, they continue to be used in weather forecasts. No meteorologist can predict the wind strength to a given mph so it is sensible to use a range related to a meaningful description. It is also quicker for a weather presenter to read a single number rather than a speed range and equally easier for the scribe to note it down without mistake.

Beaufort Scale

Force	Description	Sea Criterion / Land Criterion	wind (kt)	wave (m) mean / max
0	Calm	Sea like a mirror. Calm; smoke rises vertically.	< 1	0 0
1	Light Air	Ripples with the appearance of scales are formed but without foam crests. Direction of wind shown by smoke drift but not by wind vanes.	1-3	0-0.1 0.1
2	Light Breeze	Small wavelets, still short but more pronounced. Crests have a glassy appearance and do not break. Wind felt on face; leaves rustle; ordinary vane moved by wind.	4-6	0.1-0.2 0.4
3	Gentle Breeze	Large wavelets. Crests begin to break. Foam of glassy appearance. Perhaps scattered white horses. Leaves and small twigs in constant motion. Wind extends small flags.	7-10	0.2-0.5 1.0
4	Moderate Breeze	Small waves becoming longer, fairly frequent white horses. Raises dust and loose paper; small branches are moved.	11-16	0.5-1.0 1.5
5	Fresh Breeze	Moderate waves, taking more pronounced long form; many white horses are formed. Chance of some spray. Small trees in leaf begin to sway; Crested wavelets form on inland waters.	17-21	1.0-2.0 2.5
6	Strong Breeze	Large waves begin to form; the white foam crests are more extensive everywhere. Probably some spray. Large branches in motion; whistling heard in telegraph wires, umbrellas used with difficulty.	22-27	2.0-3.0 4.0

- wind speeds indicate the broad range in knots
- wave heights are given as probable heights - mean above maximum

Force	Description	Sea Criterion / Land Criterion	wind (kt)	wave (m) mean / max
7	Near Gale	Sea heaps up and white foam from breaking waves begins to be blown in streaks along the direction of the wind. Whole trees in motion; inconvenience felt when walking against the wind.	28-33	3.0-4.0 6.0
8	Gale	Moderately high waves of greater length; edges of crests begin to break into spindrift. The foam is blown in well-marked streaks along the direction of the wind. Breaks twigs off trees; generally impedes progress.	34-40	4.0-5.5 8.0
9	Severe Gale	High waves. Dense streaks of foam along the direction of the wind. Crests of waves begin to topple, tumble and roll over. Spray may affect visibility. Slight structural damage occurs (chimney pots and slates removed).	41-47	5.5-7.0 10.0
10	Storm	Very high waves with long overhanging crests. The resulting foam in great patches is blown in dense white streaks along the direction of the wind. On the whole the surface of the sea takes on a white appearance. The tumbling of the sea becomes very heavy and shock-like. Visibility affected. Seldom experienced inland; trees uprooted; considerable structural damage occurs.	48-55	7.0-9.0 13.0
11	Violent Storm	Exceptionally high waves. The sea is completely covered with long white patches of foam lying along the direction of the wind. Everywhere the edge of the wave crests are blown into froth. Visibility affected.	56-63	9.0-11.5 16.0
12	Hurricane	Air filled with foam & spray. Sea completely white with driving spray. Visibility very seriously affected.	> 63	11.5-14.0 > 16.0

(NB there are no land criteria for Force 11 and 12 because they are so rarely experienced on land)

Symbols Used on Meteorological Maps

Cloud Cover in Oktas

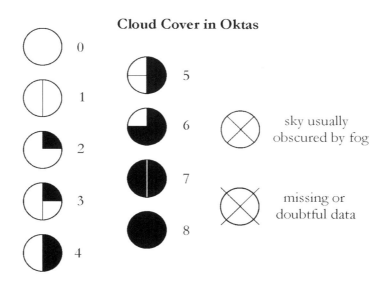

Wind in Knots

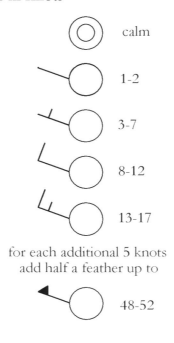

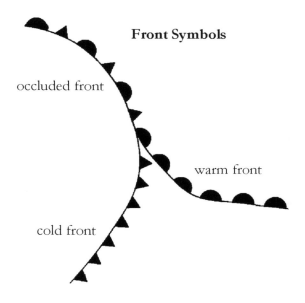

Front Symbols

occluded front

warm front

cold front

Weather Symbols

= mist

≡ fog

drizzle

rain

shower

hail

snow

thunderstorm

Glossary

Absorption	When an energy source such as radiation passes through a medium such as air it is absorbed and reduced in power by being converted into heat or some other form of molecular energy within that body.
Aquifer	An aquifer is a sub-surface mass of permeable and or porous rock or unconsolidated sediment such as sand or silt through which water can pass. Where the water collects at a low point in the aquifer it can be accessed through a well or by pump, and in some circumstances can reach the surface as a natural spring.
Back (wind)	Back or backing refers to a situation where the wind changes in an anticlockwise direction. So, when the wind moves from south-west to south it is said to back. If it moved in the opposite direction it would have veered.
Conduction	Conduction describes the transfer of heat through a material by molecular motion. In effect, as heat is applied to an object the molecules closest to the source of heat begin to vibrate and in doing so excite their neighbours initiating a chain reaction that passes the heat through the object. This is similar to the handle of a cooking pot becoming hot or the changes observed in a poker placed in a fire. Unlike convection, no onward movement of the substance or parts of the substance takes place.
Contrail	Contrail describes the cloud-like trails seen behind high-flying aircraft. It is formed by the almost instantaneous condensation of the water vapour content of exhaust gases as they leave the rear of an engine and enter the very cold atmosphere.
Convection	Convection describes the vertical motion of a parcel of air. It can either be warmer and therefore more buoyant than its surroundings and so rise or, at some distance above the surface, it can be colder and denser so that it sinks. Unlike conduction, there is an onward movement of the material, not simply a transfer of heat.
Convective Trigger	A convective trigger is any situation that encourages the initiation of heat transfer by air moving vertically. The trigger can be a thermal source such as an urban heat island or the convergence of two air masses or the forced uplift of air by a topographic barrier.
Depression Tracks	Mid-latitude depressions tend to follow a well-defined path, which can be calculated and plotted on a map.
Dew Point	The dew point temperature of a parcel of air is the temperature at which the water vapour content of the air begins to condense into water drops.
Earth's Rotation	The Earth rotates west to east around its axis.
Equinoxes	The spring and autumn equinoxes define the points in a calendar year when the midday sun is directly overhead the equator so that the hours of day and night are more or less equal throughout the world.
Fret	A fret is the local name given to coastal fog experienced along the east coast of England in summer. Further north along the east coast of Scotland it is known as haar.
Front	A front is an invisible line marking the interface between two air masses of contrasting density and temperature.

Groundflow	Groundflow describes the movement of groundwater.
Groundwater	Groundwater refers to the area below the subsurface water table where every void in the rock or sediment including pore spaces is full of water so that the zone is said to be saturated.
Haar	Haar is the local name given to coastal fog experienced along the east coast of Scotland in summer. Further south along the east coast of England it is known as a fret.
Halo	When either the sun or the moon is veiled by cirrus clouds that body is seen through the cloud as a disc surrounded by a ring of light exhibiting the colours of the visible light spectrum.
High Latitude	High latitude generally refers to that area of the Earth's surface between 60° and 90° north and south of the equator.
Humidity	Humidity refers to the amount of water vapour in the atmosphere.
Jet Stream	A jet stream is a narrow core of particularly strong airflow in the upper troposphere just below the tropopause. In the mid-latitudes of the North Atlantic this is represented by the Polar Front Jet Stream flowing west to east within the upper westerlies.
Leeward	The leeward side of any topographical feature faces away from the wind. Therefore, in the British Isles, the eastern side of the Pennines is in the lee of the hills with respect to the prevailing westerlies.
Low Latitudes	Low latitudes generally refer to that area of the Earth's surface between 0° and 30° north and south of the equator.
Mid-Latitudes	Mid-Latitudes generally refer to that area of the Earth's surface between 30° and 60° north and south of the equator.
Pressure Gradient	A pressure gradient describes the rate of pressure change in a given direction. Surface weather charts and media forecasts concentrate (without direct reference) to the horizontal pressure gradient. Although much weaker the vertical pressure gradient is not without importance.
Phase Transformation	A phase transfer involves a change in the atomic structure of a substance so that in the case of water vapour it changes under certain conditions into water drops or ice crystals. Water drops and ice crystals can transform into each other and into water vapour.
Precipitation	Precipitation includes any form of water whether it be liquid or solid that reaches the ground having fallen from a cloud. It includes rain, drizzle, hail, ice pellets, snow pellets and snowflakes. In a region where a mix of liquid and solid precipitation is received, the totals of the various forms are combined to give the annual precipitation. In such a region reference to annual rainfall – although invariably used in the media – is misleading.

Radiation	Radiation describes the propagation of energy through any medium by wave-like motions. Such movement is easy to appreciate in a body of water where energy is obviously propagated by waves moving across the surface. It is less obvious in the propagation of solar energy although we see the results in the form of heat and light. Meteorologists concentrate on three forms of energy – solar, terrestrial (solar energy reflected back from the Earth's surface) and back radiation (terrestrial radiation reflected back down to the surface by clouds).
Rainshadow	A rainshadow exists on the leeward or downwind side of a topographic barrier. Such large amounts of precipitation fall on the windward side of summits that relatively little remains to fall on the leeward side, which is therefore drier. Eastern parts of the British Isles are described as being in the rainshadow of uplands such as the Cambrian and Cumbrian Mountains and the Pennines.
Solstice	The solstice occurs twice a year at those moments in time when the overhead sun at midday is at its furthest point from the equator. This occurs in December when the sun is directly overhead the Tropic of Capricorn and in June when it is directly overhead the Tropic of Cancer.
Squall	Squall describes the sudden and often explosive arrival of a wind that is not only very much stronger than the existing wind but probably from a significantly different direction.
Stable Air	A parcel of air that is said to be stable with respect to its surroundings will not move vertically with respect to those surroundings unless subject to a convective trigger such as a thermal source, topographic barrier or air mass convergence. If it is subject to such a trigger it will, because of its stability, tend to return to its original level once the effect of the trigger has been removed. So, a stable mass of air forced to rise over high ground will tend to return to its original altitude once it has passed the summit region.
Static Electricity	Static electricity in the context of thunderstorms describes the build-up of areas of positive and negative polarity within a cloud and on the surface below.
Temperature Inversion	Temperature inversion describes a reversal of the typical regime of temperature falling with height. Although a number of inversions can occur between the surface and the tropopause it is one forming relatively close to the surface that is most significant with regard to understanding surface weather. In some situations, the temperature falls with height from the surface then begins to increase above perhaps 2-3 km before beginning to fall once more. Other scenarios are encountered so that for example, the temperature increases with height from the ground before reaching a point where it begins to fall as would be expected.

Unstable Air	A parcel of air that is unstable with respect to its surroundings will of its own volition move vertically with respect to those surroundings. It does not require a convective trigger although if such is applied the air will continue to rise once the trigger has been removed. Therefore, an unstable mass of air forced to rise over high ground continues to rise once it has passed over the summit and does not stop until there is a change in circumstances that cause it to become stable with respect to its environment.
Vapour Pressure	The vapour pressure of a parcel of air is the pressure exerted by a vapour (usually water vapour) independent of all the others gases.
Veer	Veer or veering is used to describe a clockwise change in wind direction. Therefore, when the wind moves from south-west to west it is said to veer. If it moves in the opposite direction, it would be said to have backed.
Windward	The side of any feature that faces into the wind is said to be the windward side. In the British Isles the western side of the Pennines is the windward side of the hills because it faces into the prevailing westerlies.

hopefully the weather has been demystified!

K

L

M

N

O

P

R

S

saturated air, **12**, 31,
Scandinavia, 65, 67, 76, 85, 98
Scilly Isles, 105
Scotland, 8, 16, 19, 42, 47, 57, 65, 67, 68, 69, 89, 91, 99, 104, 108, 139, 140
sea breeze, **39-40**, 67, 74, 94, 97, **106-107**
secondary depression, **51**, **108**
Severn Estuary, 99
Shetland Islands, 89
Shipping Forecast, 121, 122, 123
short-range forecast, 117
showers, 20, 55, 57, 58, 62, 63, 64, 65, 68, 69, 76, 77, 83, 84, 85, 93, 98, 99, 101, 102, 103, 108, 109, **112-113**, 117
Siberia, 71, 85
snow, 5, 11, 15, 23, 31, 62, 68, 69, 76, 93, 98, 99, **102, 103,** 140
solstice, 7, **141**
Somerset Levels, 30, 66, 91
Southern Uplands, 89
squally, 18, 54, 55, 57, 59, 61, 64, 65, 68, 101, 104, 111, 113
squall lines, **59**
St Catherine's Point, 105
stable air, 16, 24, 60, **141**
stable wave, **48-49**
standing waves, **42**
storm, 47
stratiform, 24, 26, 63
stratocumulus, 21, 25, **26**, 73, 77, 89, 91, 95, 112
stratosphere, 6
stratus, 16, 18, 21, **26**, 28, 29, 30, 53, 54, 66, 67, 69, 73, 84, 85, 88, 90, 91, 96, 112
surface pressure maps, **83-108**

T

Tees valley, 30
Tees-Exe line, 16, 108
television forecasts, **121**

temperature, 5, 6, 8, 9, 10, 12-15, 17-18, 23, 29, 31, 33, 39-41, 47-48, 54-55, 59-60, 62-64, 66-69, 71, 73-74, 76, 84, 89, 91-93, 96-98, 100-102, 106-107, 110, 115, 118-119, 122-124, 127, 139, 141
temperature gradient, 29, 40, 47, 48, 68, 96, 110
temperature inversion, **5-6,** 71, 72, 73, 77, 89, 91, 92, 95, 98, 99, 103, **141**
Thames Estuary, 2, 93, 99, 105
thermal sources, 18, 54, 59
thunder, **59**
thunderstorms, **57-62**, 65, 66, 87, **100-101**, **112-113**, 141
topographic uplift, **16**
tropical continental, 19, 63, **67**, 68, 76, 85, 97
tropical maritime, 19, 26, 29, 54, 55, 63, **66, 69**, 84, 85
tropopause, 5, 6, 11, 21, 109, 140, 141
troposphere, 5, **6**, 21, 36, 71, 140
trough (low pressure), 36, 48, **52**, 113

U

UK Meteorological Office, **115-119**, 121
UK Newspapers, **124**
unstable air, 22, 59, 63, 65, 98, 99, 102, 112, **142**
unstable wave, 49-50
Urals, 33

V

Vale of York, 30, 91
Valentia, 8, 30
vapour pressure, 11, **142**
veer, 39, 54, 55, 60, 84, 94, 96, 106, 111, 112, 139, **142**
visibility, 29, 54, 55, 62, 67, 68, 69, 97, 104, 106, 115, 136

W

NOTES

Printed in Great Britain
by Amazon